STO

COLETTE
A biographical study

COLETTE

The last years

COLETTE
A biographical study

MARIA LE HARDOUIN

Translated from the French by
ERIK DE MAUNY

STAPLES PRESS LIMITED
LONDON

FIRST PRINTED IN GREAT BRITAIN 1958

This book was first published in France under the title
Colette

Copyright © 1958
by Maria le Hardouin

This book is set in the 'Monotype' Bembo series

Made and printed in England by
STAPLES PRINTERS LIMITED
at their Rochester, Kent, establishment

Translator's Note

To avoid confusion, Colette's works are all referred to under their original titles in the chronology and the body of the text, since the titles of English versions often diverge considerably from the French. I have, however, incorporated the principal English translations in the bibliography at the end.

E. de M.

Contents

Chronology

January 28 1873: Birth of Sidonie Gabrielle Colette at Saint-Sauveur-en-Puisaye (forty kilometres from Auxerre).[1]

Her father: Jules Colette was born in 1829. A professional army officer, he was wounded in Italy in 1859, and had one leg amputated. Retiring from active service, he became tax-collector at Saint-Sauveur and married a widow, Sidonie Robineau (*née* Landoy). He died at Châtillon-Coligny (Yonne) in 1905.

Her mother: Sidonie Landoy was born in Paris in 1835 (her father, known as 'The Gorilla', was a quadroon), and lived with her brothers in Belgium before her marriage. By her first husband, Jules Robineau, a landowner at Saint-Sauveur-en-Puisaye, she had two children. Widowed at thirty, she married Jules Colette the following year, and had two children by him: Léo in 1868 and Colette in 1873. She died at Châtillon-Coligny in 1912.

[1] She was thus a few years younger than Claudel (b. 1868), Gide (b. 1869) and Valéry (b. 1871); a contemporary of Proust (b. 1873); and some fifteen years older than Bernanos (b. 1888).

Colette went to the village school at Saint-Sauveur, the village described in *Claudine à l'Ecole*, *Les Vrilles de la Vigne*, *La Maison de Claudine*, *Sido*.

1889   She passes her lower school certificate at Auxerre; what would seem to be a rather romanticized account of the hazards of the examination appears in *Claudine à l'Ecole*.

1890   Following an unsuccessful financial transaction, the family leaves Saint-Sauveur and settles at Châtillon-Coligny.

1893   At the age of twenty, Colette marries Henri Gauthier-Villars (Willy), aged thirty-four. The young couple take up residence in Paris, at 28 rue Jacob.

1895 and 1896   Two visits to Germany, including one to Bayreuth, described in *Claudine s'en va*; a visit to Belle-Ile-en-Mer.

1895   Return visit with Willy to Saint-Sauveur.

1896   At the instigation of her husband, Colette begins writing about her early years. Her first book, *Claudine à l'Ecole*, appears in 1900 under Willy's signature. In the three years after that, she publishes *Claudine à Paris*, *Claudine en Ménage*, *Claudine s'en va*.

1904   Colette publishes *Dialogues de Bêtes*.

1906 Colette's divorce. Forced to earn her own living, she becomes a mime under the direction of George Wague, and makes her first appearance at the Moulin Rouge in a revue which created a scandal. Provincial tours follow, in which she appears in several mime-plays: *La Chair, L'Emprise, Le Désir, L'Amour et la Chimère, L'Oiseau de Nuit* (this period of her life is later to be described in *La Vagabonde* and *L'Envers du Music Hall*, 1913).

1912 Colette marries again, her second husband being Henry de Jouvenel (editor-in-chief of *Le Matin*), by whom in 1913 she has a daughter, Bel Gazou. In *Le Matin*, she publishes short stories, articles and theatre criticisms. These pieces are published in collected form in several volumes: *Dans la Foule, Aventures Quotidiennes, Les Heures Longues*, written during the 1914–18 war. *Chéri* appears in 1920, *Le Blé en Herbe* in 1923, *La Fin de Chéri* in 1926, *La Naissance du Jour* in 1928. Between 1934 and 1938, she publishes *La Jumelle Noire*, a collection of theatre criticisms which first appeared in *Le Journal*.

1935 Having been divorced in 1924, in 1935 Colette marries Maurice Goudeket.

1936 She is made a member of the Belgian Royal Academy. Her reception speech is devoted to a eulogy of Anna de

Noailles, of whom she paints an unforgettable portrait. During the Occupation, she lives in the Palais Royal in Paris. Maurice Goudeket is held by the Gestapo for several months and interned at Compiègne.

1944   She is made a member of the Académie Goncourt.

1946 to 1949   She publishes two of her most attractive books: *L'Etoile Vesper* and *Le Fanal Bleu*. Her *Oeuvres complètes* appear in 1948. From 1949 on, Colette is almost completely immobilized by a painful arthritis.

1953   She is made Grand Officier de la Légion d'Honneur. The cinema discovers her: *Gigi*, *L'Ingénue Libertine*, *Julie de Carneilhan*, *Chéri* and *Le Blé en Herbe* all appear on the screen. In the theatre, *Chéri* is triumphantly revived, and *La Seconde* and *La Fin de Chéri* are staged for the first time.

1954   Colette dies on August 3rd. The Government gives her an official civic funeral at the Palais Royal.

Foreword

UNLIKE those writers who are true novelists, who preserve, in other words, a completely objective attitude (a Balzac, for example, whom one barely encounters at all in his works), Colette is present in every one of her books. This is due less, perhaps, to the fact that she sometimes transposed herself into certain of her heroines, than to the manner in which she pinned down, or rather took on the substance of, those beings who served as the spur to her inspiration. It is significant that her interest lay with certain types of individuals, and not with others. She must therefore be classed among those writers who, through the pages of their novels, disclose their own nature.

A Camus or a Malraux also belong to this same family of writers, whose personality is made manifest through their works. But their ideas develop into a prolonged and general interrogation bearing upon the human condition, and what they ask is whether this destiny has any significance or not. For Colette, with her steadfast refusal to become a writer with 'ideas', these questions do not arise, even implicitly. Her sole interest is in those relationships by which human beings deal with life in the most every-day sense. For her, the real 'human adventure' lies in the desire which draws individuals together, through all the anguish of perpetually conflicting emotions, and man's 'earthly domain' is the privileged sphere in which one has the chance to enter into the most charming interchanges with animals and plants. Our approach to such a subjective writer is bound to be one either of sympathy or antipathy. But whatever reservations we may make about Colette, it is impossible not to be moved to enthusiasm by a use of language at once so subtle and so simple, which, by revealing things to us from a hitherto unsuspected angle of vision, seems indeed to bring them into existence for the first time.

I

Snapshots

It takes time for the absent one to achieve his true shape within us. He dies, he matures, he becomes fixed.

SIDO

THERE are several Colettes. Each of us chooses the one that seems to us most like ourselves, unless, indeed, not troubling to go beyond a superficial acquaintance with her work, we limit ourselves to those epithets like 'sensual' and 'pagan' that are used all too often in any short view of her character.

For those who have barely glanced at her books and know her only through her renown, Colette is above all the author of the *Claudine* stories, in other words, a writer who, if not downright immoral, is at least tainted by a certain amorality, an impression only too readily confirmed by the social spheres described in *Chéri* and *La Fin de Chéri*. For other readers, she is the poet of the *Dialogues de Bêtes* and of nature in general, a St Francis of Assisi minus the saintliness. For still others, she is the fervent spirit of Saint-Tropez, adoring the light and the odours of the south, or the gastronome who does not hesitate to assure us, in book after book, what a large part food always played in her life. But for most of her readers, she is the novelist who through all her novels, from *La Vagabonde* to *Julie de Carneilhan*, takes as theme the eternal misunderstanding that sets those two hereditary enemies, man and woman, against each other, in a veiled antagonism rendered only the more ferocious by the fact that each can neither live with nor without the other.

Finally, there are those who seek above all the Colette who speaks in an almost confidential tone, the Colette of *La Naissance du Jour*, or the stoic and contemplative writer who appears entirely in the role of first person indicative in *L'Etoile Vesper* or *Le Fanal Bleu*.

Beneath so many diverse appearances, however, there are certain basic and invariable factors, the authentic components of her character, which both explain her work and determine it. It is these invariables that I am going to try to define, and it is the singularly vivid personality that makes itself felt at so many random points in the written work that I hope to penetrate and reveal. For in this one sees a truer Colette than the one who lived through the ordinary daily round among her fellows, and it is this personality that found itself playing to win or lose all in the mysterious gamble for fame.

*   *   *

I never actually knew Colette. I merely saw her once at the exit of a theatre, after one of the last performances she had been able to attend, thanks to what she herself called 'that somewhat bitter diversion, the invalid's chair'. Conscious of the curiosity she aroused, she held her head very erect, so as not to meet people's gaze. From the side, I could see only a pointed chin and the extraordinary wild mop of hair like a magpie's nest that concealed a third of her face. For an instant I caught the gleam of her grey eye beneath the heavily made-up eyelid, and saw the dark patches of age, like mittens, that covered the still plump hands gripping the arm-rests of the chair. She looked like some strange ship's effigy, watching the waters close over her wake as she neared the end of her life's voyage. Valéry has assured us that we make our way backwards into the future. And so it was that at the moment when I glimpsed Colette, she was already taking that last backward look that precedes the voyage into posterity.

*   *   *

Yet surely she was still, only yesterday, that slender girl swinging in a hammock and wearing a sailor costume, as she appears to us in one of her youthful photographs? What fate had in the meantime overtaken those heavy ropes of lustrous braided hair that coiled down below her knees, and the white and flowing hands?

Another photograph, this one printed in its thousands, has made us familiar with what was to be the final image of Colette, beneath a flurry of grey hair. Seated at her work table, a chiffon scarf tied about her throat, she gazes down with half-lowered eyelids at the page on which she is about to begin writing. But why allow this vision of Colette to usurp the place of all those that came before? It is the fresh countenance, at once watchful and nonchalantly drowsing, and the barely perceptible smile, that we must interrogate, as that countenance itself once tirelessly interrogated life. It is to the young girl half stretched out in her hammock and already linked in a mysterious harmony with the whole universe that we must turn. For it is the young girl who held within her those forty or so volumes that more than half a century of hard work and admirably controlled discipline were to bring slowly into being, in spite of what she herself (without thereby wholly convincing us) was to describe as her initial absence of any desire to write, her lack of a vocation.

It is this extraordinary emissary through whom Nature chose to reveal to us the hidden riches of her inner life, this budding creature who alone held the key to the mystery, the secret of genius, whom we hope to discover.

II

Early Upbringing

CHILDHOOD – SIDO – THE FAMILY CIRCLE

> *House and garden still exist, I know, but what does that matter if the magic has gone out of them, if the secret has been lost that once opened ... a world I no longer deserve to enter?*
>
> LA MAISON DE CLAUDINE

So we must begin by asking what was the true nature of this young creature in her fifteenth or sixteenth year? Native region, family background and influence, these are the things we must turn to first when it comes to explaining the circumstances which give rise to the exceptional in temperament or art. Without the house at Saint-Sauveur-en-Puisaye (the Montigny of the *Claudine* stories), without the Fredonnes woods, without the contours of certain hills, without 'that narrow and solitary valley like a cradle' which for sixteen years, she tells us, 'sheltered all my childhood dreams', and without the truly extraordinary character of the mother who is fixed forever now in our memories as 'Sido', Colette would not have been Colette as we know her, a primal force that city life was never able to detach completely from its native sources of energy.

'One never recovers from one's childhood,' Léon-Paul Fargue has remarked. For our enrichment and her own greater chance of survival, Colette certainly never recovered from hers, a childhood wholly centred within the house where 'the children (her sister with the long tresses and her two older brothers) never fought, where animals and people alike were gentle in their ways . . . where for thirty years, a husband and wife lived together without ever raising their voices against each other. . . .'[1]

In a few strokes, Colette establishes this background in its fixed and immutable outlines. 'There was no railway line in my native countryside, no electricity, no college nearby, nor any big town. In my family, there was no money, but books. No presents, but affection. No comfort, but freedom.'[2]

Only a few touches are needed for us to see Colette herself appear, for so we must already call her, her feminine-sounding surname being destined finally to supplant altogether her two first names, Sidonie Gabrielle. Delighting in the dawn, and allowed sometimes to greet it by her mother as a reward, she walks down the sandy footpath;

[1] *Sido.*
[2] *Journal à Rebours.*

it is three-thirty in the morning, and she is twelve years
old. She is absolutely alone, and she tastes the childish
triumph of being so wide awake while the others are still
asleep, and carries a basket containing a slab of bread
spread with beans soaked in wine, in which her teeth 'with
the brand new incisors' will inscribe a neat half-circle. It is
the hour, she says, 'when I became aware of my worth, of
an indescribable state of grace, and of my complicity with
the first stray breeze, the first bird, the sun still an oval,
deformed by its irruption. . . .'[1]

It is small wonder that she was aware of her secret
value. For had not her mother, as she let her go, called her:
'Beauty', 'Golden Jewel', and even 'my masterpiece'? If
exaggerated praises dull certain children, others, on the
contrary, find in them a salutary source of self-confidence
and pride. How vividly we can see her, this 'Queen of the
Earth', as she called herself, 'strongly built, rough voiced,
with two tightly-woven plaits that whistled about me
like the thongs of a whip; with hands freckled, scratched,
and marked with scars, and a boy's square forehead that
nowadays I hide down to the eyebrows. . . .'[2] Surrounded
by all the marvels unknown to town-bred children, this
young Fury was also to be observed wearing a crown of
birds. Two swallows would accompany her to the village

[1] *Sido.*
[2] *Les Vrilles de la Vigne.*

school, either nestling in her pockets or esconced in her hair, where 'they clung on with the full force of their curved, gunmetal-coloured claws'.

She was, of course, a great reader as well, and had already read much since, by the time she was seven, the *Comédie Humaine* 'no longer held any secrets' for her.[1] Apart from Saint-Simon's *Mémoires* (a volume of which her mother, with her love for the 17th-century authors, kept always by her bedside, expressing surprise that her daughter did not do the same), she had already devoured Labiche, Daudet, Mérimée, and *Les Misérables*. Soon, given the free run of her father's library, she had even made off with one of the few authors her family still tried to keep out of her reach, and had read in one of Zola's novels a description of childbirth written 'with such a crude and abrupt wealth of detail, such anatomical precision' that she fell in a faint on the grass, 'as limp as one of those little hares that the poachers used to bring, freshly killed, into the kitchen', feeling herself for the first time threatened by the fate that awaited her as 'a young female animal'.[2]

---

[1] It should be noted in passing that the three pages of analysis devoted to this work in *Mélanges* cannot fail to delight all lovers of Balzac by their depth and perspicacity.

[2] The phrase is worth noting; from remarks of this kind, scattered throughout her work, we are able to see that Colette fully accepted her destiny as a woman, and even insisted on it.

But apart from this alarm, caused by her precocious reading of a description in which she had found no reflection of her 'calm assurance as a young country girl. . . . The loves of the grazing beasts, cats mounting their females like the wild beasts their prey, the almost austere, peasant literalness of the farmers' wives talking about their virgin bull or their daughter with a child on the way',[1] nothing as yet troubled the even flow of her days. Beyond moments of unseasonable curiosity, the real Colette was 'the quiet child in whom spring already awoke a savage happiness, a sad and mysterious joy' (a joy that she was to go on experiencing, she tells us in *L'Etoile Vesper*, right into the last springs of her old age), 'a child who would exchange her toys for the first wood violets, tied with a piece of red cotton', and who, feeling herself at home and in harmony with her own body, revelled to the full in the sheer intoxication of being alive. *La Maison de Claudine*, the house of her childhood, which comes sweeping towards us like an ark on the inexhaustible flood of memory, has something in common with the jungle where Mowgli-the-Frog, the 'man-child' of Rudyard Kipling's inspiration, was brought up. True, Colette never had the privilege she would certainly have prized above all others of being brought up by Bagheera the

[1] *La Maison de Claudine.*

[23]

Panther or Baloo the Bear, but the house where fearless canaries, for the sake of their brood, would steal a few hairs from the tabby cats that sometimes went to sleep lying on top of their cage, and where the toms would breath in the full-blown violets 'with an absorbed air' and then go off to the kitchen garden to sample the ripest strawberries, was a haven where every animal, house-pet or stray, was welcomed and fed. This was the true centre for that marvel of close fusion between human and animal existence, and Colette tells us how the same sap that traverses and binds together animals and plants also stirred her own childish being, 'healthy, excited, gorged with life'.

It was Sido who held the key to all these marvels, the mother figure, the spiritual axis upon which Colette centred her own life, the conscience to which, obscurely, she was to appeal throughout her life and by which she was able to judge the weaknesses and shortcomings of her own conscience. The mother, too, was called Sidonie, but through the devotion of the one who no doubt loved her most in the world, her husband, Captain Colette, it is by the tender diminutive of Sido that she has come down to us.

To speak of Sido is already to speak of Colette: for rarely have two beings been so close, if not in mind, at least in temperament. With her tireless solicitude for

humans, animals and plants, Sido's constant preoccupation was: 'Surely this women can be saved. This child
must be looked after. But I really can't kill this animal.
...'[1] Yet at the same time, by what may seem at first
glance paradoxical, she was able somehow to accept the
inexorable law of nature red in tooth and claw. Life itself,
no matter what form it took, delighted her to such an
extent that she would have been quite ready to admit the
jubilant indifference of a Shiva, indiscriminately creating
and destroying worlds. An anecdote will show how her
mind worked in this particular way. One morning,
Colette caught her mother standing motionless and gazing
up into the sky, as if listening to some strange incantation.
'A blackbird with metallic glints of green and violet' was
busily feasting on the fruit the scarecrow had been put
there precisely to protect. ' "What a beauty he is!" murmured Sido, "do you see how he uses his claw?... And
his arrogance?... And that twist of the beak to pluck
the stone out?..." "But, mama, what about the
cherries!" Sido lowered her rain-coloured eyes to earth
once more. "The cherries? Oh! the cherries...." '
'Through her eyes,' Colette goes on, 'passed something
like a wild laughter, a universal scorn, a dancing disdain
that light-heartedly spurned me along with all the rest. It

[1] *La Maison de Claudine.*

took only a moment – and it was not the only time. Now that I know her better, I can interpret those swift changes in her expression. It seems to me that they were aroused by a need to escape from everything and everyone, by a leaping aspiration towards a law she herself had written, for herself alone. . . . Under the cherry tree, she came back to earth among us once more, laden down with cares and love, clustered with children and husband, once more kind and plump and humble before the humdrum realities of her life.'[1]

Colette tells us how 'a particular candour made her mother inclined to deny evil, even while her curiosity sought it out and studied it, mixed with good as well, with a marvelling gaze'.[2] Elsewhere, she speaks of Sido's 'blind curiosity which delighted in examining both "good" and "evil",' and of 'her skill in discovering fresh names, according to her code, for old tainted virtues and humble sins that for centuries have been awaiting their place in Paradise.'[3]

If I stress this attitude of Sido's, it is because we find the identical attitude in her daughter. For Colette as well, nothing is bad that has its place in the order of Nature; only that which is contrary to nature is evil, and that is

[1] *Sido.*
[2] *La Maison de Claudine.*
[3] *La Naissance du Jour.*

what she calls vice. Ethics, for her, begin and end there.[1]

Sido drew her spiritual nourishment entirely from curiosity and a sense of wonder. 'With certain distinguishing marks,' writes Colette, 'single or double pince-nez, a pair of spectacles, a magnifying glass, my mother was an explorer.' With her, the key word, which indeed embraced almost her whole conception of education, was: *Look!* Colette never forgot it; much later, at the end of her life, she was to say: 'We can never look about us enough, never look straight enough, never with a passionate enough intensity.'[2] The whole of her childhood revolved about this imperative: 'Look at the first bean-shoot, the cotyledon that raises a tiny cap of dried earth on its head. . . . Look at the wasp as it cuts up a fragment of raw meat with its shear-shaped mandibles. . . . Look at the colour of the sky at sunset, heralding high winds and storm. What does a high wind tomorrow matter, so long as we admire today's glowing brazier.' (Always this readiness to accept the thousand and one contradictory marvels of

---

[1] 'If I take a lover without love, simply because I know it's bad: than that's vice. If I take as lover someone I love, or even simply desire, than that's the sound law of nature and I regard myself as the most honest of creatures. To sum up: vice is the evil one takes no pleasure in doing' (*Claudine en Ménage*). For Colette, then, evil would seem to enter in only where mind appears, mind being an impure refinement, the sole cause of corruption.

[2] *De ma fenêtre.*

nature. Besides, we know how, on those famous days of high wind, when 'the cloud-swollen West' burst into white flakes, Sido would take up a brass-bound magnifying glass so that she could study more closely the finely-branching crystals of snow.') 'Look, quickly, the bud of the black iris is beginning to open! If you don't hurry, it will be over before you come. . . .'[1]

It was somewhat dangerous advice, and the child did not need to be told twice. It sometimes happened that the red earthenware bowls, filled with loose soil, in which her mother had bedded down some rare plant which should be allowed to ripen secretly, were ransacked by impatient and damaging small fingers, for, as Colette tells us, 'even in childhood, I looked for that shock, that accelerated heart-beat, that catch in the breath that the treasure-seeker knows in his solitary intoxication.'[2]

This inherited curiosity was always to be a life-giving force. When over fifty, Colette confesses that: 'It is always the same curiosity that leads me to visit one after the other, without distinguishing between them, the candle woman, the dog that can count, a rose-tree with edible fruit, the doctor who adds human blood to my own human blood, and what else besides! If my curiosity

---

[1] *Journal à Rebours.*
[2] *Sido.*

deserts me, let them bury me, for I shall no longer exist.'[1]

From Sido, however, Colette inherited not only curiosity and a passionate capacity for wonder, but also the influence of a younger, livelier, more vivacious blood than ours, a fact which would seem rather to have escaped notice. Yet Sido never concealed the fact that she had had a 'coloured gentleman' for a father. She herself referred to this unlikely progenitor, a cocoa-importer in Belgium, by the surname of 'Gorilla' that she had heard others bestow upon him in the past, and would point with satisfaction to a certain daguerreotype hanging on her bedroom wall, in which appeared, says Colette, 'the head-and-shoulders portrait of a coloured man – a quadroon, I believe – with stiff white collar and tie, a pale and scornful gaze, and a long nose above the thick negro lip that had earned him his name.' It was through this maternal grandfather 'with the violet finger-nails' that Colette received the precious gift of mixed blood which shows itself so fecund in certain individuals, the fresh response to things, the childlike vision of a race for whom being and acting are one and the same, who live in a direct relationship to nature. Coloured blood has its own strong atavism; we find it breaking through the surface in Sido's case, if only in that curious scene witnessed by the

[1] *Sido*.

twelve-year-old Colette when she unexpectedly saw her mother indulging in what appeared to be a magical incantation, spinning round like a whirling dervish, gripping her sides and uttering low moans, so as to lend her own strength to her elder daughter, Juliette, in the pangs of childbirth, the ungrateful Juliette who had broken off all relations with the family since her marriage, but whose groans were carried on the breeze over the garden wall. This manner of miming the drama, of entering into it even more, perhaps, with the body than the mind, and the semi-hypnotic gyrations, certainly mark the re-emergence of a principle at once extremely ancient and extremely obscure.

When Sido begins to impress herself on our awareness, through the loving evocation of her daughter, she is no longer the blonde young woman 'with the wide mouth and delicate chin, the grey and laughing eyes' that she had once been. She is already a woman of fifty, who has lost all her youthful attributes. We can hear her calling in the garden: 'Come here, children. Where have the children got to?' and waving the yellow wrapping paper from the butcher's with which she hopes to summon her dogs and cats about her at the same time. The more she appears in Colette's work, the older she grows, the more sharply she stands out. There comes a point when we perceive her in her final aspect, 'with her septuagenarian's small grey

plait of hair curling upwards from the nape like a
scorpion's tail', dressed always the same, like the good
housewife she was, in a dress of blue satinette drawn in at
the waist and with a gusseted bodice, a dress that Colette
was never to part with.[1] It is then that she lets fall so many
wise remarks that foreshadow the words her daughter,
too, will one day use on this same subject: 'It's a difficult
thing to preserve the characteristics of one's sex, once one
has reached a certain age. . . . Later on you'll understand
that right up to the grave, one keeps forgetting one's old
age. Even illness has no power to make one remember it.
Every hour that passes I tell myself: "I'm going to die this
evening, or tomorrow, it doesn't matter. . . . " But I don't
keep on thinking of the change that age has brought
about in me. It's when I look at my hand that I notice the
change. It fills me with astonishment not to see there the
youthful hand I had at twenty. . . .'[2]

As for illness, we know that Sido always regarded it
with horror, and found it natural enough to hand that
horror on to her daughter intact. She showed no surprise
when, having asked Colette, then aged ten, to take some
flowers to a neighbour who was ill, she saw her start
backwards, 'jibbing like an animal at the smell and image

[1] She used a piece of this dress as a binding for the manuscript of
Sido.
[2] *La Maison de Claudine*.

of sickness'. Momentarily holding Colette back by the 'rein' of one of her long plaits, Sido had suddenly exhibited, 'leaping out from behind her everyday countenance, a wild visage stripped of all constraint, charity and humanity', and had murmured with strange complicity: 'Be quiet! I know how you feel, but you mustn't say it, you must never say it!'[1] And here again, it is surely the stirring of an age-old atavism that we sense, the primitive's horror of illness and death.

When she herself was at last afflicted by illness, for a long time she refused to recognize the fact. Fighting in her own fashion against her declining powers, she began to get up earlier and earlier. 'She went on climbing and climbing the ladder of hours,' Colette tells us, 'striving to seize hold of the very beginning,' forever driven on by such 'a youthful and cunning urge for life that she managed to win over and carry along with her a body already half-shackled by death.'

Of the death of the mother she had loved so deeply, Colette tells us nothing. The extreme reticence of feeling which prevailed in all her relations with her mother, as it did indeed with all those who were dear to her – 'if I use the affectionate mode of address freely,' she confesses, 'it's more from familiarity than intimacy' – prevented her from revealing to the casual reader the depth of this

[1] *La Maison de Claudine.*

[32]

loss, one of the most painful she ever suffered. All we are told, and then only incidentally,[1] is that, having been accustomed all her life to writing to her mother, if not every day, at least twice a week, sending her letters 'crammed with bits of news both true and false, with descriptions, with boasts, with trifles, full of myself and of her . . .' she found it extremely difficult, even twenty years after her mother's death, to master the impulse to sit down, during her travels, at some hotel writing-table, throw aside her gloves, and 'ask for post-cards with views of the region, the sort that she liked'.[2] 'Why, for that matter, should I halt at a barrier so futile, so vain to question, as death?' she asks in one of the rare passages in which she touches on this subject, always avoided in her books.

All Colette tells us is that she was alarmed, during one of her mother's last visits to Paris, to see her 'so small, shrunken, feverish in her enchanting gaiety, as if pursued'. Even then, it seemed impossible to believe that death might soon overtake one who arrived 'bearing three pots of gooseberry-and-raspberry jam, the first rosebuds

[1] *Mes Apprentissages.*

[2] We can only speculate now on what Colette's letters to Sido must have been. There were more than two thousand of them. They were all destroyed, after Sido's death, by someone whose action we should like to think well-intentioned, but which was, to say the least, unfortunate.

enveloped in a damp handkerchief, and a cardboard box on which had been sown a pattern of the barometric grains of wild oats'; one who planned in a single day to 'go and buy some pansy seeds, hear a light opera, and see a collection bequeathed to the Louvre.'[1] The only presentiment Colette had of her mother's end was the day when she found that the fire had not been lit at the usual early hour in the little house at Châtillon-Coligny, when the blue saucepan in which Sido boiled her milk every morning and melted her tablet of chocolate remained hanging on the wall. But beyond these few sombre notes, which tell us what the end must have been like for such a being – for one who used to say: 'At my age, there's only one virtue left, not to hurt others' – beyond that, stretches the radiant and perfect harmony of a personality that age could never divest of its powers.

So it is that when we think of Sido, who achieved the feat of reconciling so many contradictory elements in her nature into one harmonious whole, we see her as Colette painted her for us in the days of her plenitude, so that she emerges as a being 'alternately bathed in light and shade, bowed by sufferings, resigned, fickle and generous, and adorned with children, flowers and animals like a fruitful estate'.[2]

* * *

[1] *Lune de Pluie.*   [2] *La Maison de Claudine.*

That Sido was fruitful there can be no doubt, and to such a degree that, if we did not have the example of the two sons and of the elder daughter, Juliette-of-the-long-tresses, we might almost believe that it was enough to be her child in order to become a writer whose genius, at its purest and most assured, was to spring from a profound understanding of nature and the animal world.

Yet the example of the three other children proves the contrary. Juliette's case alone, Juliette who was Sido's daughter by her first husband, 'a pleasantly ugly girl with Tibetan eyes', gives evidence that it was possible to remain wholly untouched by so many favourable elements.

'The stranger' – that is how Colette speaks of this sister with her curious kalmuk eyes, and with a quite abnormal propensity to hairiness, since the nape of her neck, her ears, 'indeed all of her faintly anaemic white flesh seemed doomed in advance to the encroachment of hair'. Forever shutting herself away in her bedroom, reading by the indistinct rays of sun or candle-light, or even by the flare of matches struck against the wall, Juliette with her eyes dilated from lack of sleep scorned the healthy and boisterous joys of the open air. She nurtured no love or friendship for anyone but the heroes of her books. An unfortunate marriage was to bring to an end the bizarre relationship she had had with her family. Although she continued to live in the same village, she would dart away

1381251

like some wayward child who fears a slap whenever she happened to meet Sido, who, after all, was still her mother. We know all about her single-minded passion for reading thanks to the unforgettable description Colette has given us of her hair. Thus we have a living picture of those abnormally long and thick tresses which almost dislocated Sido's arms whenever, armed with a whole battery of combs and brushes, she had to dress Juliette's hair. 'It was like a black curtain descending,' Colette tells us, 'as my mother unravelled each tress, and hiding her back; then shoulders, face and skirt vanished in turn, so that finally all one could see was a strange conical tent made of sombre silk in great parallel waves, parting momentarily to show an Asiatic visage, and stirred by two small hands that gropingly manipulated the fabric of the tent'.[1]

Absorbed in the vagaries of her inner drama, she remains caught forever within this strange shelter, fixed for posterity by her sister's art. Apart from this luxuriant hair, with its vague suggestion of some wild and primitive tribe, nothing else of Juliette has survived; living under the same roof as Colette, she pursued her course as a solitary star and an infinite distance separated them.

*   *   *

[1] *La Maison de Claudine.*

Then there were the other two, the two 'young savages', as Sido called them, 'the two boys, so fleet-footed, clean limbed, with no superfluous flesh', who were indeed to have an influence over Colette, by confirming her in her own streak of wildness and her taste for solitude. What was their fate to be? 'Achille, the elder, will be a doctor,' Sido predicted, 'and as for Léo. . . . Alas, poor Léo will never be able to tear himself away from music.'

At the moment when he begins to come alive for us, merged with the memories of Colette then ten years his junior, Achille, who was soon to leave Saint-Sauveur to begin his medical studies in Paris, was still a youth of seventeen. He was a handsome boy, with chestnut hair, and eyes of the same sea-green shade as Colette's, who reserved his amiability solely for his family and a few pretty girls. The younger boy, with his unruly shock of hair and pale eyes, cared only for watches and music, and would follow the strolling singers and fiddle players far outside the town, when he was not taking one of the town clocks to pieces, forever fascinated by the movement of the hands.

Both were incurably unsociable, and would allow only Colette into close intimacy with them. She would follow their long-striding expeditions into the woods, but sometimes stray off 'like a dog that likes to hunt alone, and is not answerable to anyone'. When Colette tells us later that it was by close acquaintance with cats that she learned to 'keep long silences', she might well have traced that training back to the games she had once played with her brothers, games which involved a sort of compulsory silence. The anxious Sido might well make the garden ring with her rallying cry: 'Children, come here! Where are the children?' – the solemn pines, where the two older ones particularly liked to hide, returned no answer, nor did any reply come from the lilac hedge, behind which glowed a delicate little triangular face not unlike the mask of fox or cat. Colette has three words for it when she comes to describe the loose yet so sensitive bonds that linked them together: reserve, discretion, freedom. These were the virtues the 'young savages' observed among themselves. It is clear, of course, that of the two boys, Colette preferred Achille, who, even although only her half-brother – 'but fully my brother by affection, choice and resemblance' – was to earn from her the title of: unrivalled elder. Prematurely aged by the hard life of a country doctor, traversing the roads of his small domain night and day in a light cart, finding it difficult enough to support a wife and children, and sustained only by his taste for music and the curiosity towards animals and plants that he, too, had inherited from his mother, Achille Robineau cannot be said to have enjoyed an exceptional destiny.

★   ★   ★

But what of the other, the younger one, Léo, of whom it
was thought that he would never tear himself away from
music? It turned out, on the contrary, that he managed
to escape from everything, from his chemistry studies,
the various posts he was given, and the responsibilities he
was supposed to undertake. And what can be sadder than
an 'aged sylph'?[1] That was how Colette described him
finally, 'a sixty-year-old sylph with a white moustache',
the only wonder being why he decided to live in a town
rather than to take up residence in one of the woodland
copses of his childhood. 'Ancient elf, ears plastered back
with rain' – so we see him clearly enough when, enveloped in his overcoat, 'vacant and bewitched wanderer',
he decides to pay a brief call on his sister of an evening,
not to discuss the present but rather, after opening his
watch and gazing with all the old rapt concentration at
the movement of the hands, to talk to her of some insignificant incident of their childhood, the only period
before reaching maturity in which he really belonged to
the world. With his astonishing memory, which unlike
his sister's acted as an ill-adjusted brake, he could conjure
up in the minutest detail some excursion of long ago,
some vanished garden, even the musical complaint of a
rusted iron gate which, in swinging open, would emit a
curious peal of sounds. So his thoughts would stray on

[1] *Sido.*

their vain pilgrimages, tethered forever and inescapably to an ancient stake; so he, too, remained forever incapable of achieving any success in the real world; like his brother's, Léo's career cannot by any stretch of the imagination be described as brilliant.

*　　　*　　　*

So it is Colette's destiny alone that remains a question mark. 'As for the little one . . .' Sido thought, whenever she considered the careers that might await her children, ' "As for the little one. . . ." She raised her eyebrows, interrogated a cloud, and decided the matter could wait.'[1] The waiting proved well worth while, and the delay certainly brought her no disappointment.

Behind the 'little one' stands yet another figure, but at fifteen, Colette still reserved all her conscious affection for Sido; at that age, she was not concerned with what aspects of her character she might have derived from her father.

Later, she was to ask herself what sort of a man he had been, when, in striving to distinguish the paternal from the maternal elements in her own nature, she was to discover how much she held in common with him, and to regret that, because of 'the strange shyness that fathers

[1] *Sido.*

feel towards their children', she had not shown greater perception and insight.

'Too little known! Misunderstood!' So she was to write at the start of her memoirs. A jovial man with a tune always on his lips, no one on the surface could have seemed happier than the former officer of zouaves, Captain Colette. And yet, at bottom, surely his life was the absolute contrary of all it should have been, this man who in his youth had yearned so deeply 'to die with glory and in the full public view . . . in the centre of the square, under the flag', who from being a battle veteran (he had had a leg amputated during the campaign in Italy) had become a village tax-collector and father of a family. Furthermore, it was a life that had been made only more humble and obscure by the ever-deepening and, as it were, destructive love he felt for Sido. Colette herself had only to look back on vanished pleasures, to those Sunday evenings when the whole family would return to the village in an ancient barouche ('No doubt we all looked extremely happy,' she writes, 'since looking happy was the supreme courtesy we observed towards each other'), and at once, beneath the resounding cracks of the Captain's whip, beneath his redoubled outbursts of song and all his well-simulated gaiety, she could sense now the bitter dreams of the man, how he must in imagination be still with his former comrades-in-arms as they pursued their adventures so far beyond his ken.

Behind 'his defensive snatches of song' which always 'preceded him like a breath', behind his Mediterranean gift of the gab which frequently overflowed into oaths and imprecations to which his children paid not the slightest attention, he concealed his true nature from his family. His former companions all gave instances of his extraordinary courage, but on these matters he was silent, as if recognizing that, once one has missed the only destiny one is really fitted for, one can never thereafter have any right to talk about it. Boastful and grandiloquent about so many things, on the one thing that had really mattered to him he showed a complete reserve. Later, putting two and two together, Colette was to discover what had remained concealed from her in her carefree childhood: the easily-offended delicacy of feeling that lay hidden behind what Sido wrongly believed to be 'her husband's incorrigible gaiety'. 'She thought him gay because he was always singing,' Colette reflects. 'But I who whistle whenever I am sad, I wish she could have understood that the supreme insult is pity. My father and I do not accept pity. We are not built that way. And now I am tormenting myself over my father because I know that, far stronger than all the gifts of pleasing, he had the virtue of being sad with good cause, and of never betraying himself.'[1] We know now that it was from the 'Captain' (as he was called by the entire village, out of affectionate deference) that Colette inherited this trait in her own character, just as she also inherited the habit of never speaking about those things that really mattered to her.

What she could not yet know was that to her would fall the task of vindicating another of her father's dreams – the dream of becoming a writer, which had gone side by side with the dream of dying a glorious death in battle. How was she to foresee that her life was to be devoted to writing? The following passage tells us, rather, that she was convinced of just the opposite: 'In my youth,' she declares, 'I never had any desire to write. No, I did not get up secretly at night in order to write verses in pencil on the lid of a shoe box. . . . No voice came out of the sound of the wind to whisper . . . in my ear that I should dull my ecstatic or serene perception of the universe by writing about it. . . . I felt each day more strongly that writing was just what I was not made for. . . . What felicity I tasted from this very absence of a literary vocation! My childhood, my free and solitary adolescence, both being untrammelled by any need for self-expression, were both concentrated wholly on thrusting their sensitive antennae into the world of inward contemplation, of

[1] *Sido.*

[43]

hearing and touching and breathing for their own sakes alone.'[1]

Nevertheless, from her father, she had inherited a curious passion for all the apparatus of the writing desk. At ten, 'full of base intentions', she had already begun to prowl round her father's desk, littered with all the treasures of a stationer's shop: 'Mahogany set-square, metal and ebony rulers, various coloured pencils, pens with fine or sloping nibs, bottle of liquid gum, above all the small trays of sealing wafers' of which she ate the outer tissues, but she could hardly show how greatly she coveted these requisites since the unexpected disappearance of one of them immediately brought down upon her 'the fiery gaze of a small incendiary grey eye, the eye of a rival'.

Behind one of the glass doors of the bookcase, she had cleared half a shelf on which to range her personal treasures. But soon there was no longer enough room. Sido at once showed her concern, on being told that the compartment had become too small: 'Yes, much too small, her gaze seemed to say. She's fifteen now. . . . What is to become of Minet-Chéri, bursting out of her retreat like a hermit-crab forced to leave his borrowed shell because he's grown too big? . . . Already she is escaping and I cannot follow her. Already she wants a long dress, and if I let her have it, even the least perceptive

[1] *Journal à Rebours* (*La Chaufferette*).

[44]

will see that she's no longer a child; and if I don't, under
the too-short skirt, they will see that her legs are already
those of a woman. . . . Fifteen. How can one stop her
being fifteen, then sixteen, then seventeen. . . .'[1]

Knowing the anguish she felt at seeing Minet-Chéri
reach the dangerous turning-point of adolescence, it is
easy to understand why Sido, happy to encourage what
seemed to her a childish whim, should go so far as to
steal from the 'Captain's' table the stick of gold-dusted
green sealing wax that the latter guarded so jealously
without daring to use it, merely advising Colette to hide
it with utmost care so as not to unleash the paternal wrath.

'The eye of a rival. . . .' That is the point I have been
waiting to make. For 'the small incendiary grey eye'
belonged to her father, and if he passed on to her certain
physical attributes, there is good reason to believe that he
also endowed her with certain moral characteristics. We
find in both of them a shared passion for similar objects.
One must not smile at that: other inherited traits passed
on at the deeper level were to come to dazzling fruition.
'My father, a born writer, left few pages behind him. At
the moment of writing he would fritter away his urge in
material tasks, surrounding himself with all the necessities
and even the superfluities of the writer's craft. It is because
of him that I have a touch of mania myself.'[1] It has been

[1] *Le Képi (La cire verte).*

[45]

remarked that 'the great writer merely gives expression to a certain "style", slowly elaborated and matured by a family'. Colette's case provides confirmation. The 'Captain' seemed to be filled with a curious presentiment as to the powers of judgment of a ten-year-old to whom he submitted his fragments of rhetorical prose and his odes, in which the too-obvious rhymes reverberated with awkward redundancy. Shaking her head – 'the forehead too broad to be pleasing' and the 'small rounded chin' – Colette imperceptibly let fall her verdict: 'Too many adjectives, always too many adjectives', which drove her father frantic. But even if rage drove him to call her a 'vain flea' or an 'insignificant insect', that did not shake her from her disapproving attitude. She knew, besides, that during these curious colloquies, they would some-times survey each other 'as equal and fraternal spirits'.

On the other hand, at fifteen she had no inkling of something she was to discover later: 'It was he who was struggling to emerge and relive his life when I made my first obscure attempts at writing.' Neither of them had yet grown aware of the way in which the gifts of a true writer were doubtless to be secretly strengthened by what had been the impotent aspiration of a whole life. And when he died, at the age of seventy-four, freed from the fear he had had of surviving his beloved Sido, one might well believe that all that would linger on of 'Captain'

Colette in men's memories was the pinewood coffin on which had been thrown the zouave tunic, the coffin that Sido accompanied with unfaltering step to the edge of the grave, 'so small a figure under her veils, and softly murmuring words of love meant only for his ears'. Indeed, there was to be a curious confirmation of his life's failure when his children made the discovery, on the topmost shelf of the bookcase, of a dozen bound notebooks entitled: *Les Enseignements de '70, L'Algèbre élégante, Mes Campagnes, Le Maréchal de Mac-Mahon vu par un de ses compagnons d'armes*, etc. . . . notebooks which seemed to suggest the existence of a whole lifetime's labour, but which, when opened, revealed that their hundreds and hundreds of pages of fine cream-laid paper had remained entirely blank, except for these three lines on the very first page: *To my beloved wife – from her faithful husband – Jules Joseph Colette*, in dedication of what had proved to be 'an imaginary work, the mirage of a writer's career'.

How astonished she would have been to learn that more than thirty years later, when she had already reached the peak of notoriety as a writer and her father and mother had been long since dead, a mediumistic woman friend was to say to her: 'I see behind you the spirit of an elderly man', and, having described the father's untrimmed, almost white, beard and the small eyes under the bushy eyebrows, 'Cossack' eyes, as

Colette called them, with their unbearably direct gaze, was to add: 'He thinks about you a great deal, because you represent what he himself so much wanted to be when he was on earth.' How astonished she would have been to learn that the time would come when she herself would endow her father with abounding life, through a work come finally to fruition.

*   *   *

'Their sensitive antennae' – there is a phrase over which we must pause for a moment. In truth, few people have had antennae at once more complex or more subtle. Rarely has there been an intelligence so skilled at distinguishing the various elements of hearing, sight and smell that enter into a given sensation. Marcel Proust is almost the only one with whom a comparison can be sustained in this art of translating the substance of a sensation. Talking of the school she went to, 'a sort of primitive paradise where tousled angels broke sticks to light the stove', and of charcoal foot-warmers that in winter gently asphyxiated the pupils with the scent of fruit laid upon their bars, Colette remarks: 'I believe that if some small harmless stroke of magic could restore to me, at one stroke, the aroma of apples bubbling on the grate, of charred chestnuts, and above all of that extraordinary old volume of the *New Testament*, worm-eaten, frayed and mildewed, between whose pages Mlle Fanny preserved dried tulip petals transparent as red onyx, the small grey wraiths of violets, and the spade-bearded faces of spring pansies' (the same, no doubt, that her mother described as looking like Henry VIII), 'then I believe I should be really happy. . . . I should carry off, I should breathe deep in this book of spells that reveals the past, this key that unlocks childhood once more'. . . .[1]

Looking back to her earliest years, she also remarks that: 'A child's awareness is governed by the most alive of its senses. In my case it was already the sense of smell.' And in *Mélanges*, talking of Balzac, she says: 'The little man . . . had a wild animal's keenness of scent. When he sniffs about him, I no longer dare question the view that the male sex possesses more highly skilled nostrils than ours, even though my own have little fear of any rival. . . . Often I have found myself surrounded and held at the centre of a universe that a fragrance opens and closes. . . .'[2]

So it happened that, passing a vacant lot in Paris one day, she stopped to breathe in the air long and deeply. The smell she tracked down was what she described as 'an enchanting fetidness. Emerging from rotten wood and its nocturnal phosphorescence, it also derives from the

[1] *Journal à Rebours* (*La Chaufferette*).
[2] *Mélanges*.

ephemeral mushroom, and from the mud of the gutter with its delicate muskiness, for the stream has flowed over the dried morocco leather of a tiny frog, tanned by being long dead.'

As for the smell of chocolate, its scent pervades her whole work. The first time Sido described for her the slabs of cocoa which used to dry on the roof of her father's house, where at night the cats went wild, Colette tells us that, no longer listening to the rest of her mother's speech, she remained momentarily engrossed in the perfume and the image evoked: 'The smell of the chocolate in yielding slabs, the hollow flower burgeoning beneath the paws of a straying cat.' There is almost no grief suffered by her heroines that is not appeased by the arrival of the sweet-smelling viaticum, and *Claudine* is to make a gourmand's delight of bars of chocolate melted over a wood fire on a small silver grill.

No less acute, but even more fastidious, was her sense of touch. At fifteen, returning to Saint-Sauveur from a stay in Paris, Colette mentions the aversions she felt for town apartments without gardens or animals 'where the hand, seeking a friendly caress, meets only lifeless marble or wood or velvet'. She left such apartments with their 'lack of friendly spirits . . . with senses starved and an overwhelming need to touch the living substance of pelts and leaves, of warm feathers, and the moving moistness of flowers. . . .' So she would run to the big basket over-flowing with all the cats, of every age, who had given birth during her absence, and 'sort out the mothers and their well-licked offspring, who smelt vaguely of straw and fresh milk and carefully tended fur.'

And pursuing this Jordaens-like vision of fecundity, she adds: 'Bijou, four times a mother in three years, who carried a string of new-born kittens at her teats, herself took suck, with awkward smackings of her over-large tongue and a purr like a roaring chimney, at the milk of old Nonoche, lying prostrate with pleasure with one paw over her eyes.'[1]

We seem, here, to touch on one of Colette's most essential characteristics, her passion for physical exuberance and overabundant vitality. This passion is linked, as in all those who live in close relationship with the forces of nature, with a highly developed taste for different types of food. Colette, in fact, is never misled over the quality of a particular dish or a particular wine, for has she not discovered that *boeuf à l'ancienne* 'satisfies at least three of the five senses', that white strawberries smell of ants, that there are different vintages of oranges, and does she not speak of 'the appetizing and expansive aroma of freshly-ground coffee?'

For her, as for her characters, the act of eating is as

[1] *La Maison de Claudine.*

much a source of moral as of physical energy. The heroines of *Duo* and of *Le Toutounier* are shielded against the blackest pitch of despair and the memory of their beloved dead by the joys of the table. Grilled chickens and flans and milky coffee, and the roast dripping with butter gently twice-cooked over the embers, play a large part in the moral stamina and the way of life of the characters in *Chéri*. As for the inevitable relationship between the love of good food and sensuality, we find the proof of that in Claudine's exclamation in *Claudine en ménage*: 'Alas, the sight of all that I love, the beauty of my lover, the suavity of the Fresnes forests, my desire for Renaud, all arouses in me the same emotion, the same hunger to possess and embrace. . . . Can it be that I have only one way of feeling things?'

Perhaps it was from Burgundy, with its tradition of fine cooking, that she inherited her love of good food. Colette herself puts the question: 'Where did I acquire my violent delight in country wedding feasts? What ancestor bequeathed me . . . this almost religious fervour for *lapin sauté*, for *gigot à l'ail*, for eggs poached in red wine, all served in a barn between walls hung with unbleached cloth where the red June rose is pinned in all its splendour?'[1] In spite of the vivid splash of the rose, which lifts the whole scene into poetry, the fact remains that from

[1] *La Maison de Claudine.*

childhood on, Colette discovered that in eating she experienced 'the lusty delight of feeling herself a lively animal'.

Wholly absorbed in the sensual pleasures of a small predatory beast (at least so she imagines herself), she is convinced that her desire for universal communion can be satisfied merely by touching, tasting, seeing, hearing and breathing. She seems to be entirely given over to the passing moment, and yet inside her, already, her prodigious memory has begun to store up those possessions that no one, not even the years, can ever take away. 'Life cannot rob me all that easily', she tells us later, when already in her old age. 'I shall never finish counting over all those things that chance has once made mine.' Sometimes she is aware of curious impressions: 'When I was little, a great precocious wisdom instilled into my most keenly felt delights several melancholy forebodings, which had a bitter savour far beyond my years. . . . This was . . . "the secret voice", a door half-opened, a door that for children of my age usually remains shut. . . . The voice would say: "Look, stay, this moment is beautiful! Will you ever see again, in all your life as it rushes towards you, a sun so golden, a lilac so blue in its very mauveness . . . a bed so crisp with coarse white sheets? . . . How much longer will you still be this child enraptured merely by its own life, by the simple pulsation of its happy arteries? . . . Where will you feel the first prick, the first failure? . . . Oh! make a wish to halt time, to remain still a little as you are: do not grow up, and think, and suffer! Make the wish so hard that, somewhere, a god will be moved to grant your prayer! . . ." [1]

This passage, one of the very few in all Colette's work in which appeal is made to a god, even to a pagan god, is in my opinion extremely important for the light it throws on a certain region of her soul into which she never allows us to penetrate; it gives us an exceptional insight into the depths of a being who is otherwise totally devoid of mysticism. It has sometimes been considered a useful approach to scour an author's work for the word that occurs most frequently, so as to define its dominant mood. By reversing this method, one might well characterize Colette's work by the rarity with which the word God appears in it. It is, indeed, almost absent from her forty volumes, for the simple reason that, as God neither sets off nor concludes any of Colette's trains of thought, he has no place in her universe. If it has sometimes been remarked, without undue paradox, that God is the central preoccupation of atheists, that is certainly not so in Colette's case.

Nevertheless, at the moment of taking her first Communion she had gone through the inevitable crisis of

[1] *La Retraite Sentimentale.*

religious sentimentality that all little girls undergo. But her first Communion itself brought it to an end, as is shown by this passage from *Les Vrilles de la Vigne*: 'Good old harmless *curé* who gave me Communion, you thought that the silent child gazing wide-eyed at the altar was waiting for the miracle, the imperceptible movement of the blue scarf encircling the Virgin's head?...It is perfectly true that I was dreaming of miracles, but... not the same as yours. Lulled by the incense of the warm flowers, enchanted by the mortuary scent and by the musky decay of the roses, I lived, dear harmless man, in a paradise you had no idea of, peopled with my own gods and speaking animals, with my nymphs and my goat-footed ones.... And I listened to you talking about your hell, and I thought of the human pride that made man invent eternal Gehenna for his crimes of a moment....'[1]

No doubt the young Colette, loving above all everything tangible and visible, had an innate resistance to everything belonging to the sphere of the Invisible, but the setting in which she was brought up was also at the opposite extreme from any form of mysticism: on the one hand there was 'this small free-thinking region which prefers to celebrate the New Year and as far as possible to do away with a feast that has lasted nineteen centuries and belongs to all children', on the other there was the

[1] *Les Vrilles de la Vigne.*

family background. It would be impossible to find anyone with a more lay frame of mind than the father, while
as to her 'dearest atheist Sido', who submitted to a certain
provincial conventionality by going to Sunday Mass, but
instead of the Gospel read Corneille, and was not beyond
betraying a few threatening signs of impatience for the
curé's benefit whenever the sermon went on too long,
we know that she felt a characteristic antipathy towards
any form of religious manifestation. She was full of
mocking banter and as if scandalized at what appeared to
her the absurdity of certain practices which tended to
diminish the marvels already present in the creation.
When Colette proudly showed her a bouquet of camomile and lilac which her friends in the catechism class had
told her was 'blessed' because it had been laid before the
Virgin, her mother merely broke out into an irreverent
laugh: 'Blessed? Do you think it wasn't that already?'
And Colette adds: 'My mother must have been afraid
that I would fall into the Catholic snares of incense, of
flowers, the lulling rhythm of the hymns, the gentle
bemusement of the responses.'

In that, Sido was not far wrong, for it seems clear that
her daughter would have tended not to fall merely into
the snares of liturgical 'distractions' and 'splendours'.
Colette herself confesses that she was 'a child supersti-
tiously attached to the recurring holidays of the seasons,

to those dates marked by a present, a flower, a traditional cake'....[1]

What, then, had drawn her to the catechism lessons she had followed so assiduously? Colette does not try to conceal the real reason: 'the pleasure of striking up a friendship with those one has spurned', of suddenly associating with the pupils of the Catholic school while the pupils of her own 'lay' school kept them scornfully at a distance. 'The first time that I felt another little girl's shoulder against mine, while a plait of fair hair slid down beside my own and uncoiled on my open book, while an ink-stained finger and a black finger-nail underlined the Latin text: "That's where we pick up *Ora-a pro-o nobis*", I was won over.'[2]

But there is an important qualification: 'Won over to piety? Not at all. Won over, rather, to the unknown, to the classroom refrains that were not taught at my own school, to selected extracts more impassioned than ours ... to genuflections and voluble prayers, to exchanges of pictures and rosaries, and above all to stories of "Christmas slippers".' Could there be any more striking demonstration of the mechanism, not of belief, but of credulity at its lowest and most rudimentary level? We overhear the verbal battles going on among these little girls, one side

[1] *Les Vrilles de la Vigne.*
[2] *La fleur de l'âge (Noël ancien).*

just as bad as the other: 'I tell you, Christmas is the real
holiday', – 'And I say it's the New Year that counts.' In
the end, Colette felt herself becoming less abrupt and
almost sentimental. She had reached the point of asking
her mother to tell her Christmas stories. One evening,
the latter gazed at her with those piercing grey eyes that
missed nothing, ordered her to stick out her tongue, and
as a last resource, made her drink some hot sugared wine
from her small embossed silver drinking cup. The wine
made her talkative: ' "Mama, the Gendrons' little girl,
Julotte, saw the moon come down into her sabots, at
Christmas." ' ' "Drink up your wine," ' her mother had
replied. 'She said to me, "Drink up" as if she were saying:
"Drink and talk freely." She listened to me unsmilingly
and with that sort of attentiveness I have so often seen her
give to the children.' At one moment, she even laid her
hand quickly on her daughter's arm and gazed at her so
intensely that Colette found herself catching her breath:
' "Do you believe in it? Minet, darling, do you really
believe in it? If you believe in it. . . ." '

How heavily that 'if', and the calmly detached and
meditative scrutiny that accompanied it, weighed on a
soul that perhaps asked nothing better than to unburden
itself! 'I was put out of countenance,' Colette goes on. 'A
frosty flower, that I alone could see, which hung there
tinkling in the air and was called "Christmas", began

to drift away'; we may add – drifted away forever.

Nevertheless, when at last the famous night of Christmas arrived, and from having been empty until then, now seemed as if it might contain all the mysteries, Minet had found herself awakened before daybreak by a furtive sound. In the faint glean of her night-light she saw her mother who, without coming nearer, asked in a whisper: 'Are you asleep?' To which she almost answered in all good faith: 'Yes, mama.' In front of the fireplace, Sido had soundlessly set down the small, child's sabots, which she had decorated with Christmas roses and filled with sweets and a book. But just as she was going out, a scruple overcame her. 'All at once she turned round, glided in her felt slippers over to the fireplace, picked up the two parcels by their string, and thrust the roses between two of her bodice buttonholes. With her other hand, she pulled together the straps of my sabots, tilted her head a moment towards me, like a bird, and left the room.'[1]

Clearly, Sido did not feel she had the right to assume the role of any annunciatory angel. That night passed like any other night. For a rationalist mind, there was no question of observing it as the commemoration of any decisive event. It was only on the first of January that Colette discovered, beside her steaming cup of thick

[1] *La fleur de l'âge (Noël ancien).*

chocolate, the parcels that her mother had momentarily tucked into her sabots and then taken out again. She ends the passage: 'Throughout my childhood I had no other Christmas presents but those that Sido brought me that night: her scruples, the hesitation of her pure and eager heart, her self-doubt, and the furtive tribute her love paid to the excitement of a ten-year-old child.'

On a certain spiritual plane, a door that had barely opened had thus been closed again forever. But since Colette had arrived at adolescence, the mother's anxious vigilance had only grown sharper. Whenever 'the child dawdled on autumn evenings, gathering mushrooms or mauve colchicums, those "lights of autumn",' Sido, 'like a broody mother bird on the edge of the nest', would stand waiting on the doorstep, peering up and down the street for her return. Then, taking down the 'Captain's' overcoat from the hallstand, a child's cape or a blue apron whose strings she would tie under the chin, she would loom up before Colette, returning from her stroll, as the very personification of uneasiness. It was because she had all the time been following this fifteen-year-old daughter 'with the long hair, the supple waist, the small cat-like face with the wide temples and pointed chin'. 'So, in the evening,' Colette tells us, 'under the green dome of the hanging lamp, a grey-eyed gaze, so sharp as to be almost harsh, would scan me up and down, studying

me from my scratched cheek to my muddy shoes, assess-
ing the damage: a streak of blood on one cheek, a tear
near the shoulder . . . shoes like sponges. . . . So that's
all. . . . Thank God, once more, it's nothing more than
that.'[1]

But how much longer would it last? And under what
guise would come the danger threatening from outside?

[1] *Journal à Rebours.*

III

The Formative Years

WILLY — THE METAMORPHOSIS

There is always some danger in the mysterious
attractions of those whom we do not love.

BELLA VISTA

In the small house at Châtillon-Coligny, forty kilometres from Saint-Sauveur, where Achille was now practising as a doctor and where the whole family had gone to live following an unfortunate turn in their affairs, there seemed little likelihood of any unforeseen development. The golden and straw-coloured countryside, capped with airy and dark-hued woods, was almost as much like a Dürer water-colour as Colette's own native region. Each member of the family stood ranged round 'the youngest one', so that it seemed her life would still be sheltered for a long time yet. But it was not for nothing that her mother's anxious solicitude had been awakened. Colette was indeed on the verge of the most momentous encounter of her life. In a few months, she was to meet for the first time Henri Gauthier-Villars, the son of a publisher of scientific works with whom Captain Colette, as a member of the Geographical Society, already had an acquaintanceship. Fifteen years older than Colette, Henri Gauthier-Villars was destined to have a decisive influence on her art, partly by encouraging her to give expression to it, even if only with the object of making money, and partly by imposing upon it a certain style from which Colette was only able to free herself subsequently by the force of her genius.

At first sight, it was a completely paradoxical, even an absurd conjunction, this coming together of two people who had not a single thing in common. She was a young country girl, a true child of nature, direct, simple, out-spoken. He was a man-about-town already growing stout, happy only among the city streets, in social and literary coteries, pre-eminently a complex and artificial creature.[1] There is something bewildering about such a crying contrast. Yet we may perhaps glimpse the truth in the phrase in which Colette one day revealed her mother's genuine innocence in contrast to her own: 'Sido did not realize that a particular animal may wish to die, that a particular child may seek out corruption, that a

[1] One should not overlook the fact, however, that beneath so much artifice there was a genuine taste for music. He was one of the first to understand Wagner's operas and to defend them in France, in his *Lettres de l'Ouvreuse*, which enjoyed a considerable reputation at the time.

closed flower may ask to be opened and then trampled underfoot.' For that matter, Willy with his flat-brimmed hat, the lower part of his face concealed behind 'richly curling and spiky blond sideburns' and an 'imperial' which gave him a vague resemblance to Edward VII, could no doubt pass for a handsome man in the period around 1900. Nevertheless, this is how Colette was to describe him later, in *Mes Apprentissages*: 'I have known certain enormous individuals. Monsieur Willy was not enormous, but convex. His bald head (elsewhere she speaks of it as 'pink, boundless and powerful'), his prominent eyes, the short and shapeless nose between low-slung cheeks, all his features followed a curved line.' And when she discovered, behind the outward appearance of the charmer, 'the shadow of a man already getting on in years, the clouded, indecipherable gaze of pale blue eyes, an awe-inspiring capacity for tears, a marvellous huskiness of voice, a fat man's strange lightness of tread, and the hardness of an eiderdown stuffed with pebbles', she merely concluded: 'What a lot of contradictory riches, of varied snares. . . .'

The character of Maugis, in the *Claudine* books, allows us to round off the physical and moral portrait of Willy: 'All aglow with paternal vice, a lover of women, of foreign liqueurs and plays on words, amateur hellenist, musicographer, scholar, swashbuckler, sensitive, devoid of scruple, jesting as he hides a tear, thrusting forth a stomach rounded as a bullfinch, calling young women in their underclothes "baby", preferring the half-undressed to the nude and a sock to a silk stocking.'[1] From the portrait of Maugis, we can, in fact, glean some idea of the emotional outlook and bearing of the man she had married.

From this point on, there are no further faithful renderings of settings and people. From now on, all we shall find – with the exception of *Noces* and *Mes Apprentissages*, which appear to be autobiographical – are merely fragments of a transposed reality, scattered at random throughout her work.[2] Speaking of her labours as a writer, Colette herself tells us[3] that, over a period of many years, what she sets down on paper is 'what I know about myself, what I try to hide, what I invent, and what I guess about that knowledge'. So here, too, it is through a great many contradictory snares that we must choose our direction.

*　　*　　*

But why, precisely, did it have to be Willy? In part, no doubt, it was the glamour of the mature man for an

[1] *Mes Apprentissages.*

[2] In the *Claudine* stories, *Les Vrilles de la Vigne, La Vagabonde, La Retraite Sentimentale.*

[3] *La Naissance du Jour.*

inexperienced young girl, the prestige of Paris over the provinces, the prestige of the writer and the busy journalist for one whose impatient young life seemed to unfold a shade too slowly. In the pages of *Noces*, Colette reveals that she came finally to feel a tender admiration for the 'very Parisian journalist' who, having become a friend of the family, would visit them from time to time at Châtillon-Coligny. Besides, how could she remain insensible to the importance she acquired from the attentions, at first amused but soon heightened by desire, of a man whose principal aim in life was women? In *Noces*, we learn how, after an engagement lasting two years, at the age of twenty she became Willy's wife. Colette was already seventy when her memories of that 15th of May, 1893, appeared. Even after the passage of fifty years, they remain extraordinarily fresh and sharply defined:

'With my white train caught up over one arm, I went down into the garden alone. The fatigue of a day that had begun early, after a night given up to waking dreams, at last settled down upon me.' She tells us specifically that she was married at 1.30; and the ceremony itself was a simple one. No mass was said, merely a benediction. There were no guests, apart from the witnesses, but plenty of masculine faces wearing the customary beards, composing a stiff group entirely in the manner of a Douanier Rousseau. Now everyone seemed intent on making the occasion as ordinary as possible. The 'Captain' had settled down to read in his armchair. The bridegroom and Achille, in shirt-sleeves, were trying to work out anecdotes for a daily paper that Willy was then directing. As for the bride, in her muslin dress gathered in at the neck and waist, a white ribbon tied round her hair in the manner of Vigée-Lebrun, and her long plaits swinging against her calves, she had seated herself on one of the front steps, her mind a blank, yet secretly waiting for something. Suddenly, we find Colette making this unexpected confession: 'The exaltation of a young girl in love is neither so sustained nor so blind as she would like to believe. But pride compels her to maintain a brave silence, even at those moments when she is most ready to give her genuine feelings timely expression, in a great cry of awakening and fear.' 'That cry never rose to my lips, for two long years of being betrothed had settled my fate without in any way changing my life.' It was really the idea of a threatened independence that brought the wish to cry out in fear; Gauthier-Villars would no longer return alone, on the wretched slow train to Paris, the next day; he would be accompanied by the very young bride who, all day, had suffered 'the embarrassment of living under the gaze of one who was weighing up his chances.'

Colette sought out Sido. But the latter, 'in her dress of

coarse silk with jet trimmings, her face reddened as it was when she was unhappy', turned away. (Colette tells us later that Sido always felt 'a vast maternal revulsion' from her daughter's emotional life.)

Sido, then, offered her no comfort. During the meal, the bride nodded to sleep like an over-tired child. The final disclosure comes swiftly afterwards: 'The next day, a thousand leagues, abysses, discoveries and irremediable metamorphoses had cut me off from the past.'

'Metamorphosis' – no other word could more aptly describe the change wrought in Colette's way of life. I must pause for a moment at this important juncture. For Willy was just as vital to her as Sido had formerly been: without them, Colette would not have become the person revealed to us by her art.

Sido and Willy were the only two major influences that brought themselves to bear on Colette's life. If those two influences were contradictory, they did, nevertheless, have one thing in common, and that is that neither was in any sense transcendental.

'It was with this fighting cock that my mature life as a woman began,' Colette exclaims. And indeed it was a terrible sentimental education to be introduced to love by a Willy! For Colette, steeped in her native region and brought up by Sido in that sort of peaceful provincial existence that always sets considerable store by preserving a good name, it meant, in fact, having to undergo an extraordinary transplantation. From the very start of her marriage, she became the object of a subtle experiment designed to remove all trace of the old Colette. Now, she was produced as a curiosity, the 'savage' to be exhibited in the drawing-rooms and coteries of Paris. Willy, in fact, put Colette on show as a means of augmenting his own publicity. For was he not the first to supply the special numbers of the literary reviews with piquant anecdotes on the couple's domestic life, since the latter must be kept in the public eye? It is therefore no cause for surprise that Willy, 'who left no stone unturned', did not scruple to accentuate to the point of scandal the embarrassing impression created by his appearances at the races or the theatre accompanied by Polaire, who played Claudine in the stage version of *Claudine à l'Ecole*, and by Colette with her hair now cut short, her eyes enlarged with make-up, the two women dressed from top to toe in identical costumes, with the express purpose of making people take them for twins, and of underlining a deliberately equivocal degree of intimacy between them. The sight of this bizarre trio gave rise to considerable public disapproval, which found expression in insulting remarks. Colette certainly underwent a harsh apprenticeship!

'Will the reader understand,' she asks, 'that to change from my country girl's existence to the life I led from 1894 on was an adventure calculated to drive a child of twenty to despair, if it did not make her drunk with elation?'

Willy had chosen an extremely dubious anvil on which to hammer out a new personality for one who (whatever her feelings of curiosity and even her secret audacity, the imperative claims of a temperament nourished by abounding good health and zest for life) remained nevertheless unspoilt in mind and sensibility.

*   *   *

The pages Colette devotes to Willy in his role as initiator[1] show him in what appears to be an impartial light. She warns us, besides, that anyone who sees any long-standing grudge in her remarks is mistaken: 'After an interval of thirty years and more, a woman who has had to be reborn from her ashes more than once no longer feels either passion or bitterness, but only a sort of cold pity and an unindulgent mirth, which resounds as much at my own expense as at the expense of the chief subject of this study.'

Highly jealous of his reputation as a writer, and exaggerating his physical appearance to conform with that role so that everyone might know and recognize him, Willy was indeed an outstanding personality. The façade of the man-of-letters was a borrowed one, since more

[1] *Mes Apprentissages.*

[70]

often than not he had not himself written the books he set his name to. Nevertheless, Colette assures us, he had more talent than all the hacks whom he asked, either for payment or out of friendship, to elaborate for him some 'outline' that he felt incapable of dealing with successfully himself. And if, as a writer, he suffered from a form of agoraphobia of the blank page, on the other hand he was highly skilled in the formidable art of getting hold of money by one means or another. It was only when he enrolled Colette in his literary factory, on the same footing as his other hacks, fully grasping how much she could help his output of novels, that the young woman saw him as he really was, a man whose true nature she had been far from perceiving in her provincial isolation. It is rarely that Colette gives us a more detailed psychological portrait, even although she tells us that no one could ever really know 'this man who, all his life, pretended to be poor. The delights he revelled in,' she goes on, 'were quite incomparable. For not only did he conceal the true extent of his possessions – that is only human – but he borrowed from the poor as well. He took pleasure in the bitter savour of a writ of attachment, and would surrender to the bailiffs – like a thickly-fleeced sheep that escapes through the thorn enclosure at the price of a few tufts of wool – a few threadbare flannel vests, an old pair of trousers, and some fraying collars, the rest being safely stowed away under another name. . . . At little outlay, he gained a name for being extravagant and a gambler, and cut a great dash at Monte Carlo losing five-franc counters.'[1]

Whatever the real Willy was like, and although Colette tells us she was never sure whether he should be called Machiavelli or Fregoli, the fact remains that she was to live with him for thirteen years.

*　　*　　*

No doubt the greatest peril, among all the 'various snares' of which Colette speaks, in this ill-matched union, lay in what must have been both a revelation and a harmony in the realm of the senses. The fact that the *Claudine* books are written in the first person does not entitle us to regard them as autobiographical, and Colette herself refuted that suggestion: 'Claudine is not my double.' Nevertheless, we learn that Claudine's husband, Renaud, who is much older than herself and loves her in a half-libertine, half-paternal fashion, delights in 'the confidences of mirrors . . . lights suggestively lowered'. Certain expressions have an unmistakably authentic ring. 'For him, gratification comes joyfully, smoothly and easily, while me it prostrates and engulfs in a mysterious despair that I solicit and fear at the same time.' There are yet other phrases that must arise out of genuine experi-

[1] *Mes Apprentissages.*

ence: 'sensual pleasure came to me as a devastating and almost sombre marvel', or again: 'Renaud initiated me into the secret of pleasure given and received, and I revelled in it passionately, like a child with a lethal weapon.'[1]

Of this delicate transition from her life as a young girl to being Willy's wife, we have an even more direct account in *Mes Apprentissages*, a book which deals with certain phases of Colette's life. It was written when she was about fifty, and memory having already gone through the process of distillation, she is able to use a freer tone. But by a method dear to her, in order that her observations may not be too personal, she generalizes by presenting them in the third person.

'There are many girls of barely marriageable age who dream of becoming the object, the plaything, the licentious masterpiece of a mature man.' Or again: 'A burning sensual intrepidity throws too many impatient young beauties into the arms of seducers already half-vanquished by time. The corrupter need not even set any price to it, his impetuous prey has no fear. Often she even demands in astonishment: "And what happens next? Is that all? Can't we at least start all over again?" So long as her acquiescence or her curiosity persist, she has no clear picture of her mentor.'[2] And then comes the disen-

[1] *Claudine en Ménage.*   [2] *Mes Apprentissages.*

[73]

chanted, if not actually bitter, confession: 'Disgust has never been any obstacle. That comes later, like a sense of integrity. Disgust is not something women shrink from.' Without any help from psychoanalysis, Colette has perceived perfectly clearly the link that may exist between disgust and desire. Furthermore, it is surely because 'taste' and 'distaste' spring from an almost common source in human consciousness that Colette is able to put the question: 'Who can discern whether we do not attach ourselves more firmly to what repels us than to what attracts us?'[1] What was formerly farthest removed from one may eventually become one's most faithful reflection; and that was the risk that Colette ran as a young woman. In *Claudine en Ménage* (written during her years of marriage to Willy), the heroine, casting a backward glance at herself, observes: 'Within myself, I feel the advance of that agreeable and gradual corruption that I owe to Renaud. Viewed through his eyes, the big and serious issues of existence shrink and dwindle away, while useless and, above all, harmful trivialities assume an enormous importance. But how am I to stand firm against the incurable and captivating frivolity which carries him away, and me with him?'

*   *   *

[1] *Chambre d'hôtel.*

Why should one lay so much stress on this first experience of love? For the simple reason that it influenced the
whole of the novelist's work, itself inspired wholly by
love. Colette herself tells us that there was a good deal of
justice in the reproach her second husband was to make
to her subsequently: 'But can't you write a book that
isn't about either love, or adultery, or some half-incestuous
attachment, or a broken affair? Isn't there anything else in
life that matters?'[1] Since the extraordinary Willy, she
tells us, 'possessed the gift, and employed the tactics, of
keeping a woman's thoughts ceaselessly occupied, indeed
several women's thoughts, of marking them out for his
own and maintaining a sway over them not to be con-
fused with any other',[2] it is highly probable that she herself continued to bear his imprint.

If the Colette of the 'animal' stories, of plants and of
nature, is based wholly upon her childhood at Saint-
Sauveur, Colette the novelist has her origin in those
thirteen years she spent with Willy. Furthermore, there
was more to it than merely the physical bond; on her
side, at least, there was certainly love as well. On Colette's
second marriage – an occasion which Sido regarded with
the same grave suspicion as the first – we find the latter re-
marking: 'Fortunately, you're not in any great danger!'
Commenting on the significance of this ambiguous

[1] *La Naissance du Jour.*   [2] *Mes Apprentissages.*

phrase, Colette explains: 'In her view, I had already gone through what she called the worst moment in a woman's life: the first man.' Colette herself concludes: 'A woman only dies but once,' and we suddenly glimpse how deep her own feelings must have run. Certain passages in *La Vagabonde*, written in 1910, four years after she had divorced Willy, and at a time when as a dancer and mime, she was experiencing all the hardships of life in a touring music-hall show, allow us to perceive how greatly she had been attached to her first husband. 'Heavens! How young I was, and how much I loved him, and how much I suffered!... After the first betrayals, after the revolts and surrenders of a young love that stubbornly continued to hope and endure, I set myself to suffering with a pride and a tenacity that nothing could deflect.' It is true that the 'vagabond' divorces her husband because, after an over-long period of patience and submission and a revelation of herself as a member of 'the true female breed', she eventually decides that it is better to risk hardship, even to the point of suicide, rather than continue to live with the man who has caused her so much suffering. 'No longer to suffer the nightly vigil,' she writes, 'no longer to lie awake with one's feet freezing in the bed that is too big, no longer to dwell upon those plans of revenge that emerge out of the darkness and swell to the beating of an angry heart all smarting with jealousy, then are pricked by the clink of a key in the lock, and cravenly subside as soon as a familiar voice exclaims: "What? Not asleep yet?" Oh, I had had enough. One can't make a habit of jealousy.'

This is one of the rare passages in which Colette speaks at length of a sentiment she must have known only too well herself, and of which nowhere else, not even in *La Seconde*, does she give a more subtle analysis. The whole art of the writer lies in not forcing the substance of his own experience into immediate use, in not transcribing it at the moment when it is at white heat. At all events, that is one of the cardinal principles of Colette's method of creation.

In the only phrases in which she allows herself to speak of regret, it is also through Renée Nérée, the vagabond, that she utters them: 'You found me once, says love that knows no pity, now you must lose me forever. . . . I took from you those things that you can only give once: trust, the religious wonderment of the first embrace, the freshness of your first tears, the flower of your first suffering.' One cannot mistake the impassioned accents. It is true that on another occasion, Colette was to exclaim: 'Can you see chance turning me into one of those women entirely bounded by a single man, so much so that they take with them into the very grave the embalmed artlessness of an old maid. Just to imagine such a fate would make my fleshly double tremble, if it were still capable of trembling, at the retrospective peril,'[1] so that we can but speculate on the novelist Colette would have been if she had been allowed to remain faithful. But in *Mes Apprentissages*, looking back on that period of conflict and suffering, she also tells us: 'What a nuisance it was, to have monogamous blood flowing through my veins!... Must my love be a matter of staying in my place, of waiting and still waiting? When love is experienced truly for the first time, it is not easy to say: on that day, through that fault, it died.'

One thing certain is that over a period of many years she was a docile wife, and that one of Willy's most frequent injunctions found her obediently and promptly bent upon her task: 'Quickly, my dear, quickly, there's not a sou in the house!' 'Quickly,' Colette tells us, 'I wrote the four volumes of the *Claudine* stories, *Minne*, *Les Egarements de Minne*.... But at *La Retraite Sentimentale*, I jibbed.'[2]

For it was indeed Willy who, some eighteen months or two years after their marriage, was to utter the fateful words: 'You ought to jot down on paper some of your memories of your first school. Don't be afraid to throw in any savoury details, I may be able to make something of

[1] *La Naissance du Jour.*
[2] *Mes Apprentissages.*

it. We're low in funds.' And although Colette tells us her first feeling was one of extreme boredom, she adds: 'On the corner of the desk, with the window behind me, one shoulder hunched and my knees twisted round, I set about writing industriously and in a mood of indifference.' At a stationer's, she had discovered the familiar school exercise books, and 'the cream-laid pages, with their grey-ruled lines and red margin', brought to her fingers 'a sort of reminiscent itch of school impositions and the tranquil sensation of fulfilling a commission'.

What she had begun to write was the manuscript of *Claudine à l'Ecole*. At first, Willy was disappointed, and did not see how he could turn it to account. But a few months later, coming upon the exercise books in the drawer where he had locked them away and reading them through once more, he suddenly leapt for his hat and rushed off to his publisher.

'That was how I became a writer,' Colette concludes simply.

That was in 1900. For the next fifty years, she was to go on writing without a pause.

IV

The Claudine *Stories*

THE BACKGROUND TO COLETTE'S NOVELS
TAKES SHAPE

Love is not an honourable sentiment.
LA NAISSANCE DU JOUR

'I KNEW how to climb, whistle and run, but no one ever came and suggested I should make a career of being a squirrel, a bird or a doe. The day that harsh necessity put a pen in my hand, and that, in return for the pages I had written, I received a little money, that day I realized that on every other day thenceforth I should have to continue slowly and obediently writing, patiently reconciling cadence and syntax, rising early because I preferred to, going to bed late because I had to.' Colette concludes this particular passage: 'That is all the young reader of either sex needs to know about a writer deliberately vowed to a wise domestic obscurity behind the sensuous surface of the novel....'[1]

Sensuous is certainly the word for Colette's early

[1] *Journal à Rebours.*

[80]

novels, almost as if through a quirk she was loath to
abandon. Referring to *Claudine à l'Ecole*, Willy had
advised her: 'Put a bit more spice into these childish
situations. For example, Claudine and one of her friends
could be drawn together by something more than just
friendship . . . do you see what I mean?'

His meaning is perfectly plain: and Colette from then
on followed his advice. 'Nothing is more reassuring than
a mask,' she tells us. 'The origin and anonymity of
Claudine' (the whole series appeared, in fact, under
Willy's name, thereby greatly enhancing his literary
notoriety, since he passed himself off as 'the father of the
Claudines') 'amused me as would a slightly indelicate
farce, and I was quite ready to introduce a piquant note'.

Colette confessed later that she had no great fondness
for her first book, nor for the three that followed it, and
her judgment of them remained just as severe as the years
went by. For these heroines 'are too indiscriminately
childish and madcap in their ways . . . and show a complete indifference to the harm they cause'. 'In twenty or
thirty years,' Catulle Mendès had warned her, 'you'll
discover what it means to have created a type in literature.
It's a sort of punishment that pursues you. . . . An intolerable recompense that one spews forth.'

'Why did I not create a type more worthy, by virtue of
simplicity and naturalness, of enduring!' Colette was to

exclaim, and time will doubtless prove her judgment correct. If we ourselves judge these works harshly today, however, that is not, perhaps, solely for the reasons Colette has given us. The character of Renaud, for example, struck her as 'more hollow and light and empty than those spun-glass balls one uses to decorate Christmas trees, and which shatter into quicksilver fragments in one's hand.' But apart from this character's lack of psychological unity from one book to the next, and the fact that the gentle and reticent Renaud of *Claudine à Paris* should not also be the seducer of *Claudine en ménage*, nor the hero who dies in fraternal and reconciled mood in *La Retraite Sentimentale*, these novels all suffer from the directive laid down by Willy, which was: to arouse the reader's senses and to kill as many birds as possible with one stone. Hence, under the pretext of tracing a young girl's adventures as she discovers life through the first stirrings of passion, the introduction of those subsidiary characters whose primary purpose is to inflame and excite. Thus, lurking in the wings in all these novels, we find characters like 'that silken flotsam', Annie, a young woman perpetually on the look-out for a lover, and Marcel, the young pervert of sixteen, who although still a schoolboy, is portrayed in the guise of a Charlus avid for youthful flesh, and already, like some elderly rake, corrupting his class companions. Colette used homosexuality as a bait in all her novels up to *La Vagabonde*, which appeared in 1910. It crops up with monotonous regularity, like a nervous tic, to contribute its share to the deliberately equivocal atmosphere. As for the principal heroine, we are made well aware that from her first appearance in *Claudine à l'Ecole* (by far the best of the series, since it is set against a country background which allows breaths of fresh air to enter this aviary of young schoolgirls, caught in all the turmoil of puberty), she has no fear of any experiment, either masculine or feminine.

What is already striking in these early novels is that, in the absence of any true awakening of the heart, what the woman looks for always is sensual pleasure. The heroines of the Claudine stories up to *La Retraite Sentimentale*, the Annies and the Minnes, are far from being sweet young things; on the contrary, their sole preoccupation is the satisfaction of their sensual appetites through a repeated series of falls from virtue. 'It's my body that does the thinking for me,' exclaims Annie. 'It's far more intelligent than my mind.' In this universe of purely physical sensation that Colette evokes for us, insinuation, or rather, according to Monsieur Willy's formula, 'the half-dressed rather than the nude', introduces a further element of perversity.

One finds a number of passages in poor taste in these early volumes, which are a further reason for their weakness. The social sphere which forms their background has become a thing of the past without achieving a style of its own, the fault lying, no doubt, in an excessive over-simplification of character: for these characters are psychologically constructed so as to appeal only to that chance reader indefinitely multiplied that one calls 'the great public'. To that extent Willy had made no mistake about achieving the desired aim: the largest possible sale. The scabrous nature of the subject matter, as it seemed at the time, and the audacity with which these emancipated young women demanded the same sensual freedom as men, dispensed with the need for any deeper psychology.

Then, struggling towards us through this throng of pleasure-seeking women and these men whose only mission seems to be 'to unleash the small, wicked, unscrupulous beast in every woman', come the first two reassuring emissaries of the animal kingdom, freshly descended from that ark from which all Colette's beloved animals will later emerge, the only two representatives of purity: Fanchette the cat and Toby-Dog.

From the moment that Colette reverts to her true self, she discovers once more what is noblest in her own being: her communion with nature and the animal world. The closing pages of *La Retraite Sentimentale* are impregnated with this life-giving force, and it is these pages that make the book seem better than it is. They open a breach through which we can escape far from the human intrigues that have failed to hold our interest. Similarly, at the end of *Claudine en ménage*, we find ourselves confronted by the only truly essential character in the book: childhood. Returning to Montigny, after her shared love affairs with Renaud and Rézi, Claudine exclaims: 'Sitting on my small boat-shaped bed, the smiling welcome of my childhood bedroom floods me with tears, tears as transparent as the ray of sunlight dancing among golden coins on the window-panes. . . . I have been hurt, but perhaps the hurt will do me good? I am near to thinking so, for indeed, I cannot be entirely unhappy here at Montigny, in this house.' Sitting at the foot of a walnut tree, she feels as if she herself is becoming a tree, and one is tempted to add, 'once more': this return to nature liberates her from all human impurity, and restores to her her former innocence.

These impressions are not far removed from what Colette might well have felt at fifteen. Yet, while she laboured away at her task like an obedient pupil (from *Claudine à l'Ecole*, for which Willy had employed every possible means of publicity, the success of her novels had been prodigious and it was a question of exploiting a successful formula), the years had slipped by. Colette herself tells us how many: 'I was thirty. An age at which one has already acquired . . . the strength that makes for

survival. . . . An age at which one is no longer prepared
to die for anyone, or through anyone. Already there is
that hardening that is rather like the effect of a petrifying
spring.' But in that, she was mistaken. 'The powerful and
sensual genius who creates and nurtures the visions of
childhood,' a genius that, according to her, gradually
fades into extinction as we get older, in her case never
died. For six months in the year, she would break away
from Parisian life and the marital apartment where
Willy entertained all the women he liked, and escape to
Franche-Comté, to the house at Monts-Boucons[1] that
Willy had liberally handed over to her so that her literary
output might be increased. There, apart from his 'visits
of inspection', she enjoyed 'a solitude such as the shepherds
knew', between the bulldog, Toby, 'ecstatic or expiring
with emotion', and the angora rabbit, Kiki-la-Doucette.
She was changing, but it was certainly not in the direction
that an unscrupulous mentor would have desired. 'While
I was writing *La Retraite Sentimentale*, I was developing
powers that had nothing to do with literature. . . . I was
changing. What matter if it was a slow process! The
essential thing is to change. . . . I was waking obscurely
to a sense of duty towards myself, the duty to write
something other than the *Claudine* stories. And bit by bit,
I delivered myself of the *Dialogues de bêtes* (which she

[1] It was to become the Casamène of *La Retraite sentimentale*.

obtained permission to publish under her own name), in which I accorded myself the pleasure – not a keen but at least an honourable pleasure – of not talking at all about love.' And she adds: 'I did not return to putting love into a novel, and taking pleasure in it, until I had regained my respect for him – and for myself.'[1]

Years later, recalling the time when, like other anonymous acolytes, she had laboured 'in Monsieur Willy's workshop', Colette was to confess that it had been nothing more nor less than a gaol, the key being turned in the lock, and freedom restored four hours later; and then only on condition that one could show, not 'a clean pair of hands, but pages blackened with ink'. Nevertheless, the window was not barred, and she could easily have slipped from her 'leash' if she had wanted to. Thus, when those years of application and of melancholy were finally ended, she asked herself: 'Can one learn how to live, then? Yes, if one dispenses with happiness. Beatitude teaches one nothing. To live without happiness, and not waste away in the process, there's an occupation, almost a profession.'

It was this 'profession' of dispensing with happiness that gave her novels their characteristic tone, for with two exceptions,[2] all are concerned with the theme of failure in love.

[1] *Mes Apprentissages.*   [2] *Mitsou* and *Gigi*.

Then came the day, in 1906, when the words: 'All is over!' were pronounced by 'the man who first laid claim to me', and without fuss or drama, but also without hope of appeal, the separation took place 'with a reasonableness, a hushed atmosphere as though snow lay on the ground'. When the divorce came through, she found herself installed alone in a small ground-floor apartment in the Rue de Villejust, the cat and the dog for company. A new life was indeed beginning. But Colette could never forget the initial shock, nor condone it. She was faced with every disadvantage. She had to work to earn her own living. Her literary reputation was nil. The public were familiar only with the name of Willy: she had to force them to accept Colette. During those difficult years, her taste for independence grew steadily stronger. In 1906, divorce was still regarded as a scandal. Nevertheless, Colette courageously accepted a double burden of social disgrace, first by being a divorced woman, and secondly, by becoming a mime in a touring music-hall show in order to earn her living.[1] Her music-hall years were the final decisive influence on her character. Her later ups and downs (setting aside old age itself, which in her case was to assume such a particular significance) had no effect on her work.

[1] In *La Vagabonde*, she remarks: the music-hall is the profession of those who have no profession.

Reckoning the cost of those thirteen years, Colette told herself as she stared at her own reflection in the mirror: 'What I have lost is my pride, the certainty I had of being a child singularly endowed, and of feeling within myself an extraordinary soul, a soul full of masculine wisdom, ready to burst the bonds of my frail body. Alas, I have lost almost all that, to become, after all, just another woman. . . . Who was it who cut my Cybele's tresses?'[1]

The one who had cut those tresses could fade from the picture; but as the instrument of that painful revelation that there is a total antimony between pride and love, between the ardent certainty of childhood, the only age in which the absolute can dwell, and the compromise one is forced to accept later as the only way to get on in life, he bequeathed to Colette many of the features that were henceforth to form the background to the world of her novels.

[1] *Les Vrilles de la Vigne.*

V

From La Vagabonde *to Colette's other Heroines*

Not even the most beautiful countries of the earth will I look upon, when they appear in miniature in the amorous mirror of your glance. . . .

COLETTE was indeed to return eventually to the theme of love, but without ever being able to treat it with quite the old degree of respect. The exaltation she had once felt when, with each fresh dawn, it seemed to her that love regained possession of the world, had given way now to a secret self-contempt, a contempt for the servitude in which woman is linked to man and man to woman through certain habits rarely avowed, but which she was too lucid to disguise, as most people do, under flattering self-deceptions. Having escaped from the tyranny of the senses and of jealousy, she had no desire to fall so swiftly back into the trap. All the distress of feeling oneself held captive, she expressed through the 'little dog' who says to her mistress: 'I remember how solemn I suddenly felt,

[90]

and that overwhelming tenderness that made me settle myself wholly on one of your outstretched hands. . . . There was an end to it: I loved you. I savoured the hopeless melancholy of cherishing the one who loves you . . . and the terrible fear of losing that which one has scarcely hoped ever to possess.'[1]

'One is despoiled by everything one loves,'[2] Colette was to write on another occasion. It is a bitter observation which runs like a leit-motif throughout her work. It is to escape this inevitable deprivation that Renée Nérée, taking her lesson from a first unhappy experience,[3] and becoming a music-hall artist, prefers from then on to have nothing to do with love, rather than surrender her liberty a second time. Beneath the thinnest of disguises, Renée Nérée's struggles and rebuffs are undoubtedly those of the novelist herself.

In *La Naissance du Jour*, Colette looks back over the dominant theme of love as it runs through all her work, and shows us how it found expression through certain of her feminine characters in the following sentences: 'On the bluish paper,' she tells us, 'I set down some chapter devoted to love, to sorrow for past love, a chapter

---

[1] *La Paix chez les Bêtes.*   [2] *Bella Vista.*

[3] A relationship with a certain Adolphe Taillandy, for which the original model does not seem far to seek, and for whom, she tells us, adultery was only one of the forms – and not the least delectable – of falsehood.

completely dazed by love. I gave myself the name of
Renée Nérée, or else, by a premonition, I drew the
portrait of a Léa.' Thus it is left to *La Vagabonde* to
express the highly sensitive feeling for independence
which now begins to appear freely in Colette's work.[1]

The craving for freedom underlies the entire action of
La Vagabonde. Instead of returning, at the end of a theatri-
cal tour, to the rich and affectionate suitor who wants to
marry her, she leaves him forever with the words: 'For
a long time I shall think of you as one of the temptations
I have had to face on my way!' She chooses to sacrifice
him for the sake of solitude and freedom, for 'the hard
but agreeable life of a mime and dancer', for a basically
honourable decision to be self-supporting.

[1] In *Mes Cahiers*, for example, there is this entry dating from the
year 1908: 'I am forced to admit it, the tour captivated me by
combining the attractions of unexpectedness, hope, irresponsibility,
and curiosity perpetually satisfied and perpetually renewed. I am tired
and sunburnt even before the arrival of summer, my hair has lost its
lustre . . . and yet I keep thinking: When shall I set off again? When
shall I resume the life of a licensed Romany, watching steeples and
forests and rivers drift by?' Two articles entitled *Là-haut* and *En
Ballon* (*Dans la Foule*) also convey to us Colette's keen and wholly
physical pleasure at feeling herself without ties, entirely possessed by
a hunger to explore unfamiliar territory. Yet one should also note, in
Mes Cahiers, this passage: 'I love the thrill of each fresh departure, and
yet surely some vestigial ghost of myself still haunts the chimney
corner', a passage indicating that her attachment to certain places
must always have been a bar to her nomadic impulses.

Yet how difficult she finds it to stifle that childish impulse to run and hide in the arms of a protector: 'But shall I also be able to overcome, for it is a hundred times more dangerous than the sensual animal, the forsaken child that trembles within me, nervous and weak and so ready to stretch out its arms and cry: "Don't leave me alone!" That part of me fears the night and loneliness, illness and death, and when evening comes, draws the curtain over the frightening blackness of the window-pane, and grows listless with no other sickness but that of feeling itself insufficiently loved. . . .'

How difficult it is, too, to fight against her own physical impulses! 'How is one to escape? . . . The first obstacle that besets me is the body of a woman lying prone across my path, a body made for pleasure, the eyes shut fast in a voluntary blindness, the limbs outstretched, and ready to perish rather than abandon the source of its delight. That woman, that creature whose only object is pleasure, is myself.' ' "You are your own worst enemy!" How well I know it, dear God, how well I know it!'

It is here that Colette gives us one of her finest descriptions of physical passion, descriptions which, in fact, are fairly rare in her work: 'I have not closed my eyes. I knit my eyebrows threateningly at the pupils that stare down at me, endeavouring to subjugate, to extinguish my own. . . . The kiss stirs, importunes, crushes down, then retreats,

assumes a rhythmical movement, then pauses as if awaiting a reply that does not come. . . .' (Elsewhere she speaks
of 'two flowers slowly crushed together, in which the sole
movement is the palpitation of two commingled pistils.')
'All at once, involuntarily, my mouth submits to being
opened, irresistibly parts and opens as a ripened plum
bursts open in the sun. . . . From my lips down to my
flank, down to my knees, the old imperative anguish
quickens once more, radiates outwards, the throbbing
wound that longs to open and find release in opening once
more, the forgotten sensual bliss. . . .'

The temptation to abandon herself completely is great.
But Renée Nérée has no illusions: 'He has no thought for
my happiness, only for his desire. The fierceness of his
desire for me hampers him like an encumbering weapon.'
The woman recognizes her ancient adversary in the man
who hopes one day to possess her. But she also knows that
'in the limitless desert of love, sensual pleasure holds a
burning yet a very small place'. Thus, in her own fashion,
she spares the man who loves her by refusing to yield to
him. 'Dear intruder, you whom I wanted to love,' she
tells him in her farewell letter, 'I leave you with your sole
chance of growing in my estimation: I am going away.
. . . Are you not the one who thinks he gives, yet seizes all
for himself? You came to share my life. . . . Yes, *to take
your share of it!* To play an equal role in all my actions.'

*　　*　　*

*To suffer ... perhaps, after all, it's an undignified
way of filling in one's time.*

LA NAISSANCE DU JOUR

La Vagabonde stands quite apart from the rest of Colette's
work. The whole book is filled with her presence, like
the bellying sails of a ship leaving port. The angle of
vision changes in the works that follow, from which the
novelist deliberately abstracts her own personality. For if
her own taste for independence was to become more and
more marked, on the other hand, she was to endow all
her later heroines with the subservient status she herself
had rejected. As she herself tells us, she had already,
during the early years of her apprenticeship, acquired her
chief skill, 'which was not a skill in writing, but the
domestic art of knowing how to wait, to dissimulate, to
pick up crumbs, to mend and stick together and restore
the gilt, to make a good bargain of a bad one, to lose and
win back in the same instant the frivolous joy of being
alive.' All Colette's heroines are gatherers of crumbs; it is
their function in life to 'conceal, obliterate, forget', and
all of them share in that limitless resistance with which
women confront suffering.

The heroine of *La Vagabonde* has already told us: 'A
woman hardly finds it possible to die of grief. She's such
a strong animal, it takes a great deal to kill her. You

[95]

imagine she is wasting away with grief? Not at all. Far more frequently, this creature, born so weak and sickly, emerges from the struggle with an indestructible nervous strength, ennobled by an inflexible pride, an art of patient dissimulation, and a sovereign contempt for those who are happy. In suffering and dissimulation, she grows strong and supple as through a daily and highly dangerous form of gymnastic exercise.' And Renée Nérée concludes that people are quite wrong when, speaking of some woman's powers of endurance, they exclaim: ' "She's made of iron." What they should say, quite simply, is: "She's a woman," and leave it at that.'

This has already been enough to show the ethical outlook Colette bestowed on most of her heroines. But from now on, we must take note of a further phenomenon. The *Claudines* have already accustomed us to a deliberate pursuit of pleasure. From *La Vagabonde* onwards, as soon as Colette's ardently amorous heroines discover that pleasure, they become wholly subjugated to the man who provides them with it. Speaking for herself, Colette tells us, in *La Naissance du Jour*: 'In matters of sensual pleasure, my eyes were always bigger than my stomach,' but it is a very different matter for the women portrayed in her novels. The heroine of *Le Képi* is perhaps the most striking example. Marco has 'adopted' a young soldier, much younger than herself, with whom she falls in love. Before that happens, she is a sensitive and serious-minded woman; but once in love, she seems to lose all intellectual grasp, and even to stop thinking altogether, as she succumbs to an erotic fixation.

From this point on, the whole cycle of Colette's novels, from *La Chatte* to *Julie de Carneilhan* and including *Le Blé en Herbe*, *La Seconde*, *Chéri* and *La Fin de Chéri*, revolves about the deceptive relationship by which a man and a woman are bound together; a relationship whose only truth is based upon the claims of the senses, which alone are not likely to lie, unlike the heart and the emotions, these being invariably shown by Colette as non-existent the moment desire has vanished. More often than not, love is no more than a physical coming together between two partners, or rather two adversaries, who keep a mistrustful watch on each other. They cannot achieve intimacy and understanding on any but the physical plane, and even then they continue to be locked in an underhand and sometimes bitter struggle, devoid of any respect for each other.

This struggle begins with the first onset of adolescence, and in *Le Blé en Herbe*, we see how the two fifteen-year-olds, Vinca and Philippe, tormented by the lurking passion that drives them together while their families are spending a seaside holiday in Britanny, gradually abandon the realm of friendship for less innocent diversions.

We are struck by the delicacy of nuance, the art with which the smallest shifts and changes in a person are observed, at the moment when that person reaches (one is tempted to say 'sinks into') the state of greatest plenitude and self-fulfilment: the state of being in love. Everything is already potentially present in these children of fifteen: the man's pursuit and blind attack, and what will later become his disillusionment and lassitude as well, and the woman's instinct to wait, passive and sly, a prey existing in the world only to be devoured.

Vinca, with her short hair 'dishevelled in straight golden strands' and 'her beret discoloured as a sand-dune thistle', is caught at that ambiguous age when a young girl seems to hesitate over whether to be a girl or a boy. When she goes fishing for shrimps, she tucks up her skirt to reveal 'two long brown legs with well-shaped knees' with 'the serenity of a small boy', yet it is a woman's destiny that lies before her nonetheless. From time to time, 'the fury of childhood' still intrudes, bringing a merciful respite, between herself and Phil, but already she must learn the grown woman's gift of remaining silent, and suffering for what she conceals. And when she appears before Phil in a sudden rage inspired by love, all restraint gone, 'scarlet with wrath . . . her mouth flushed and dry, her nostrils flaring with her angry breathing, her eyes like twin blue flames', and begins to shout at him, 'giving easy rein to her feminine fury, like a petrel riding the storm', that only leads her more securely into the blind trap of her future womanhood, with its impotent and sterile rages. To her young companion belongs the risk, the freedom, the possibility of changing; for her there is only 'the mission to endure that has fallen to the lot of all the female species, and the noble instinct to take up residence in misfortune by exploiting it as if it were a mine full of precious ores.' One day, it is true, she almost gives way to a gesture of despair, but when she discovers that she has a rival, abruptly a new bond attaches her to life: 'You need not worry, Phil! I'm not going to kill myself because of that woman. Six weeks ago . . . Yes, then I let myself go right down into the depths. But then, it was for you I was going to die, and for myself. . . .'[1]

Here we are taken right into the heart of the feminine mystery. It is the knowledge of a rival that spurs and vivifies her. For Vinca, the die is already cast: the only thing now is to know whether she will be capable of fulfilling the only destiny open to a woman, which is to shore up the fragments of happiness, concealing her true

---

[1] This is a sufficiently significant passage to be worth relating to the passage in *Mes Apprentissages*, in which Colette tells us that on the discovery of her husband's first infidelity, she, who after the brusque transition from the country to the city had at first gone into a sort of languishing decline, was now suddenly and urgently possessed by what she calls 'the desire to endure and to fight back'.

feelings, using her guile with her master, and consenting to wait for him always.

★   ★   ★

We are to see the same struggle, which has already started in the realm of childhood, manifest itself once more between two beings barely emerged from adolescence in another of Colette's novels, *La Chatte*, in which she succeeds in placing in the foreground all the dignity and mystery of the animal, in a universe in which man himself is a hopelessly impoverished creature. The story relates simply how a young couple is split up by a third 'person' – there is no other word for it – the cat, Saha. The young wife, Camille, is jealous of the way her husband constantly pampers the cat, 'the small blue pigeon, the pearl-grey demon', which he has introduced into the household as a rival, or rather, as its true mistress – for Camille herself is merely an intruder. Saha alone is the 'aristocrat': that is Alain's term for her. One cannot imagine anything more banal than the young couple, whose dreams never rise higher than a winter sports holiday or a two-seater sports car. One knows that their conversation consists solely of platitudes, that here are two people who fail totally to understand one another. Camille nevertheless believes she is gaining a hold on her husband's affections, 'for she noted with pride how, increasingly, Alain wanted to possess her'; she is unable to perceive that this 'act of possession was accomplished almost angrily, a hasty coupling of two bodies, from which he would thrust her away, breathless, seeking the fresh side of the open bed'. There, in his renewed solitude, 'he was free to probe down into the sources of what he called their incompatibility. He was wise enough to perceive that those sources lay outside the sphere of frequent physical possession' and 'would trace them back to those fastnesses in which man's hostility towards woman remains forever fresh and unaging'. For Alain, indeed, there is no possible companionship except with the cat.

Even without word or gesture, the man's tender feeling for the animal is all too apparent, and one day, referring to Saha, Camille cannot refrain from uttering the word 'rival'.[1] 'Rival,' Alain at once thinks, inwardly addressing the words to Camille, 'how could she be your rival? You can only have rivals in your own impure world.' In his eyes, indeed, woman is fated to corrupt in all her dealings, whereas Saha, on the other hand, belongs to the

[1] In *La Paix chez les Bêtes*, we find the opposite case of an animal manifesting jealousy of a human being, when the dog says to the young woman who has stolen its master's affections: 'No, you will never know how at one moment, I wanted to leap up and fasten my teeth in your throat, and cling on there, and listen to your blood murmuring like a stream.'

[101]

realm of the 'pure'. To her alone belongs the role of pure friendship.

One evening, everything comes to a head. The scene of the drama is a balcony overlooking Paris, at the top of a nine-storey building all of concrete and glass. It is one of the finest passages in all Colette's work, and is worth quoting in full:

'One July evening, when they were both awaiting Alain's return, Camille and the cat were resting on the same parapet, the cat recumbent on folded paws, and Camille leaning there with her arms crossed. . . .

'They exchanged a glance, merely investigating each other's presence, and Camille did not speak to Saha. She leaned over, as if to count the series of orange awnings unfurled at intervals from top to bottom of the steed façade, and brushed against the cat, which got up to make way for her, stretched, and lay down again a little farther along.

'Camille yawned nervously, straightened up, took a few absent-minded steps, and leaned on the parapet once more, forcing the cat to jump to the floor. Saha stalked off with dignity, and made to go back into the room. But the door had been closed, and she sat down with a patient air.

'With a far-away look, Camille stood there motionless, her back turned. Nevertheless, the cat was watching

Camille's back, and its breath began to come faster. It got up, turned round in a circle two or three times, interrogated the closed door . . . then it gave vent to a long, disconsolate miaow, and Camille spun round.

'She was a little pale, in other words, her make-up stood out clearly on her cheeks as two oval moons. She forced the cat, with a threatened kick, to jump up once more on to its narrow observation post. . . . Saha had recovered herself, and would have died rather than utter another cry. Pursuing the cat without seeming to see it, Camille moved backwards and forwards in complete silence. Saha waited until Camille's foot was almost upon her before leaping on to the parapet, and then sprang back on to the floor of the balcony only to evade the outstretched arm that would have hurled her from the nine-storey height.

'She was methodical in her flight, carefully judging each leap, keeping her eyes fixed on her adversary. Acute emotion, the fear of dying, brought the sweat out on the sensitive pads of her paws so that they left an imprint of flowers on the stuccoed balcony.

'Camille seemed to weaken first, to slacken in her malevolent intent. She glanced at her wrist-watch. . . . Saha, sensing her enemy wavering in her resolve, hesitated on the parapet, and Camille, thrusting out both arms, pushed her into empty space.

[103]

'She had time to hear the claws scratching at the plaster, and to see Saha's blue form, twisted into an S-shape, snatching at the air like a trout leaping upwards, then she drew back and flattened herself against the wall.'[1]

When the husband returns, carrying Saha in his arms (for, after bounding down from awning to awning on to the lawn, she has miraculously escaped death), there is only one thing left for the couple: to separate. Alain thinks, with a feeling of relief: 'Now we can be silent, and sleep, and breathe without each other.' Camille, for her part, is at last ready to be conciliatory and to make a place for Saha. But Alain judges her coldly: 'How easily she accepts everything I find intolerable . . .' he reflects. 'Already she's organizing things, weaving her web, putting out feelers, already she's picking up the pieces, patching things up. . . . It's terrible.'

We have been given a vivid insight into the total lack of understanding that may exist between two human beings. There is only complete solitude in a closed universe, with no possibility of escaping outside it.

*   *   *

Again, in *La Seconde*, we find people who remain entirely

[1] *La Chatte*.

in the dark about each other. When Fanny, the present wife of 'Big Farou', asks him if his first wife was intelligent, he replies in all sincerity with the highly revealing phrase: 'I never knew her really well, you know.'

But the essential theme of the book is the acceptance by a wife of another woman in the house, not so much as a rival, but rather as an ally who 'seconds' her in the difficult task of satisfying a man.

Here, all the different themes of servitude are intermingled. Fanny has already grown accustomed to her husband's infidelities. Nevertheless, when she discovers that Jane, her husband's secretary, who also helps generally about the house, Jane whom she had regarded as her friend, has been deceiving her as well, she experiences a momentary revolt. Yet what is she to do, a young woman avid for every pleasure, among which the pleasures of the flesh are certainly not the least delectable? What is she to do, when she has already caught the habit of pleasing men precisely by 'a slave's spineless compliance'? What is she to do, when her main occupation lies in 'poring with gentle antelope's muzzle over a pack of cards' and working out the same game of patience twenty times running?[1]

---

[1] Many of Colette's heroines – such as Camille and Gigi – spend most of their time at cards, when they are not engaged at their principal sport: men.

In short, how can she go on rebelling for long against the man on whom she is dependent? Fanny instinctively knows the role a woman must adopt, and she quickly settles into 'an attitude of docility, of keeping her feelings hidden. . . .' The man, 'with his yellow eyes', has only to allow his large features to crease with laughter again, and she herself drops her voice, 'seeing the rich red of his open mouth', and assumes the look of the 'cherished handmaiden', the attitude of 'slavish compliance'. How many times in the past, in her fever to serve, Fanny has kissed his hand, with its 'slight velvety down like a leaf of sage', while the man generously surrenders his hand to the almost timorous caress.[1]

As for Jane, she asserts that she gave in to Farou only because she knew what small importance Fanny had hitherto attached to her husband's infidelities. But she has never had any feeling of friendship or moral esteem for anyone else but Fanny. 'Thank heavens!' she exclaims, 'you were there as well. . . . You were there at the same time. . . . One feels so alone with Farou.' If Fanny insists,

[1] A short story called *La Main* (in *La Femme cachée*) shows us how much servility Colette's heroines can put into this sort of kiss. A woman waking up next to the man she has just married notices his hand on the sheet, 'red and ruddy-haired, with squat thumb'; hiding her fear and disgust, 'and starting on her life of duplicity and resignation, of vile and delicate diplomacy, she bent down and humbly kissed the montrous hand'.

she is prepared to leave quietly. But Fanny begins to reflect: 'In a week's time, he would have found someone else . . . he's bound to go back to his pet Mohammedan idea of happiness . . . but can I start sharing my life again with someone else? Two of us are none too many to live alone with Farou. . . . Standing up to Farou!'

For Colette's heroines, the essential thing seems to be to preserve at all costs a pampered yet ever precarious existence. Jane will not leave. Indeed, seeing her old friend's solicitude, Fanny only just masters the sympathetic impulse to take her in her arms and embrace her 'in the egalitarian confusion of a harem'.

Whatever one's first impression may be, *La Seconde* is not a true study of jealousy, and barely even a love story: it is the story of an alliance between two women against the man they love, the eternal bestower of solitude.

In *Mes Apprentissages*, Colette shows how such an alliance can be formed. Referring to Charlotte Kinceler, who had been Willy's first mistress, she notes: 'It was from her that I got the idea of tolerance and dissimulation, of acquiescence in a pact with the enemy. . . . Lotte and I became, not friends, but intrigued by one another, matching courtesies like a pair of reconciled duellists.' And drawing the moral from her experience, she concludes: 'I gained the certitude of my own flexibility, for so I have always named my control over myself, considering that

[107]

no human resistance can last, unless we know how to bend.'[1]

*　　*　　*

In her struggle against man, there is no question of the woman gaining the upper hand, but she can at least endeavour, by dissimulation and cunning, not to be totally vanquished. Camille was too young and too impatient, and thus failed in the task. The same fate is to befall Edmée, the young wife of 'Chéri'; lacking sufficient docility, she fails to win her husband.

In the whole of Colette's work, it is only the women who live by their charms who escape from bondage: their role is to subjugate the male. They are saved by the intelligent direction of their own interests, and a wholesome and enlightened cupidity. It has been said that 'all dreams are of the flesh', but when love has become an activity with a fixed price, the flesh ceases to dream at all. Nothing could be more prosaic than the lives of Léa's *demi-mondaine* friends, or of Gigi's mother and aunt and

---

[1] Here one must refer to the following passage from *Ces plaisirs*: 'Succeed, as I have done, in diverting the force of love, so that it may be put to serve some other egalitarian fever! ... When there is renunciation agreed upon between two women, and one concedes to the other the prestige of the bed, the atmosphere about them takes on an insipid nursery odour, a smell of dubious protectiveness, of herbal infusion in which orange blossom assumes the function of masking the sprig of artemisia. ...'

all the women in their circle. The poetry of dreaming flesh is to be found only in Mitsou. Through the love she has begun to bear for Lieutenant Bleu, we sense, as it were, the groping motions of a frail antenna which is struggling to break free, to assert itself as tenderness and intelligence.

*   *   *

From this analysis of a number of Colette's novels, it is already possible to perceive the essential features of her work as a whole. It has been alleged that in her characters, masculine psychology is explored less deeply than femi-nine: but Camille is no more complex than Alain, nor Vinca than Phil. As for Julie de Carneilhan, can one properly speak of complexity in her case at all? Her only moments of true happiness are those she experiences in the company of a man, even when it is a man she scorns. The latter has only to show a twinge of jealousy on her account, and she is once more absorbed into 'a world of keen and simple pleasures, in which the woman, as the object of men's rivalry, bears their suspicions with ease, listens to their insults, undergoes various assaults, and is presumptuous enough to hold her own with them'. That, surely, is the course of action that Camille and Madame Farou have laid down for themselves. In this world where the claims of the flesh rule supreme, it is always one and the same gesture that has to be accomplished between a man and a woman, so that no one can claim to be unique: for all are interchangeable.

In *Ces Plaisirs*, a book which Colette devoted with cold lucidity to sensual pleasure, we are told that a woman in love cannot tolerate in the man any feeling other than his feeling for her. In reply to a question from Colette about the friendships he might have had in his life, Damien, that inveterate old Don Juan, exclaims angrily: 'Surely you can see! ... They'd never have put up with it!' We sense the male acrimony against the female, a sort of ghoul who feeds on the very substance of the one who has the weakness to love her. As the inexhaustible Damien lets us more and more into his confidence, some small light is thrown upon the prison in which this physical love is played out, between partners as greedy to take as they are incapable of giving. What these obsessed creatures lack, Colette reflects, is any outlet by which to communicate with the outside world. 'In all that weight of feminine flesh, no draining channel, no vent for clean air to enter. ... All love affairs tend to create an atmosphere of dead-lock.'

At the opposite extreme from this conception of love, one thinks inevitably of André Suarès, of that passage in which is expressed the certitude that love is not within the reach of men, and that man shows himself at his most derisory and grotesque precisely when he allows himself

to fall into the trap of desire. 'Far from being the serf and
slave of nature,' he tells us, 'passion destroys nature in the
great lovers. For in a great love, instead of being the passive female, the doe that grazes peacefully on the flowery
meadow while the males kill each other for her sake, the
woman chooses her beloved at least to the same extent
that she is the object of his choice. A single love is the rule
for a woman endowed with a great passion, and to life
without that love she prefers death a hundred times.'

With Colette, woman is always the doe that grazes on
the flowering clover. As for carnal possession, 'holocaust
to which I give only reluctantly the name by which it is
jestingly called pleasure', if it leads certain of her heroes to
wish to relinquish life, that is not, as with Tristan and
Isolde, through a desire to rise above themselves, but
through the weakness of natures fated to an incurable
mediocrity.

That is the case with the hero of *Duo*, Michel. If he
kills himself when he discovers his wife has been unfaith-
ful, it is not because his love aspired towards greatness,
towards an impossible absolute, but on the contrary,
because of an almost sordid motive. His entirely physical
jealousy drags the world and the woman he loved so
deeply into the mud, that he is left with no other loop-
hole but suicide.

* * *

COLETTE

Chéri and La Fin de Chéri

Uncomprehendingly, he suffered a double disorder.
At times he capsized, was borne lightly along, as if
empty forever.

MES CAHIERS: CLOUCK

Although written earlier than the novels we have just
been discussing, *Chéri* and *La Fin de Chéri*,[1] which can be
considered as a single work by virtues of the steady
deepening of the characters' psychology, provide both
the prefiguration and the ultimate image of the particular
human type whose tragedy is never to have looked into
his own heart, and who can therefore never really know,
or even guess at, the reality of another person.

But at least, considering the environment in which
Chéri is placed (the world of expensive courtesans in the
years around 1910), we find nothing surprising in the
nullity of these creatures, as we have been surprised by
the nullity of the artists and middle-class couples who
haunt *La Chatte*, *Le Blé en Herbe* or *La Seconde*, whose
complete lack of curiosity, of any general view of the
world, and indifference to anything outside their own
banal lives, deprives them of any sort of distinction.

In *Chéri* and *La Fin de Chéri*, we are confronted with an
'illiterate élite', with a sort of 'aristocracy of the under-

[1] Published in 1920 and 1926 respectively.

[112]

world', which fills us with astonishment for the opposite reason.

The son of a courtesan, Chéri has grown up 'by turns forgotten and adored, among faded chambermaids and tall sardonic men-servants'. The beauty which, even in childhood, has made American women single him out and call him 'little masterpiece', reaches perfection as he comes to manhood: 'Hair with the bluish sheen of a blackbird's plumage, a smooth, hard chest, curved like a shield . . .' – there is the portrait we are gradually given of him, with the added note that anger widens his dark eyes, 'gleaming with insolence behind the bristling eyelashes, and parts the chaste and disdainful curve of his lips'.

Each morning, although he is barely more than twenty, he submits his beauty to a rigorous inspection in the mirror, on the alert for the encroaching wrinkle, like a man of property jealously making an inventory of his possessions. He has all the coquetry, the vanity and the brainlessness of a pretty woman, and if he were not already in possession of considerable wealth, owing to the wise investments made by his courtesan mother, there would be only one word to describe the childish and imperious impulse that makes him demand presents of jewellery from the women who succumb to his beauty.

His marriage to the daughter of one of his mother's

rich friends – financial considerations being the only ones in which he does not take honour lightly – has interrupted his liaison with Léa who, at forty-nine, is coming to the end of 'a successful career as a richly rewarded courtesan, and as a good-hearted creature whom life has spared both from flattering catastrophes and exalted sufferings'.

At first glance, nothing could be more banal and sordid. But in the actual writing, the story is built up by a series of touches finer and deeper than any to be found in novels like *Duo, Le Toutounier,* or *La Seconde*. What is also perhaps unique in the whole of Colette's work is the lyricism that runs through every page, a lyricism that gleams and flashes whenever the author is willing to give it free rein. A scene such as the one in which we discover Léa in Chéri's arms closes with an image of classical beauty: 'Nevertheless, she foresaw with a sort of terror the moment of her own undoing grow nearer, and endured Chéri as she might a torture, warding him off with hands grown weak, and imprisoning him between her strong knees. Finally, she gripped him by the arm, gave a feeble cry, and sank into that abyss from which love emerges pale and speechless, with a deep longing for death.' A beauty like that with which Colette has endowed her hero is enough in itself to add dignity and a hidden dimension to the book, thereby lifting it above the mediocrity of its subject-matter. Chéri as we discover him in bed would not be unworthy to take his place among those figures as they appear, barely emerged from the swirling trails of matter, on the roof of the Sistine Chapel: 'His bare torso, broad at the shoulders and slender at the waist, emerged from the rumpled sheets as if from the waves, and his whole being breathed the melancholy of perfect works of art.'

No one could be more a stranger to himself than Chéri. Here he is as he looks at Léa 'with that force and fixity of vision that make the gaze of the puzzled child or the suspicious dog so formidable. An indecipherable thought appeared in the depths of his eyes, whose shape and dark wallflower hue, whose hard or langorous gleam, had served him only to win love, never to reveal himself.'

Léa calls him her 'naughty baby'. In the arms of this still beautiful woman who 'loved order and fine linen, wines in their prime and carefully planned meals', this woman who has doubtless meant more to him than a mistress, something of a mother as well through the tenderness she alone has lavished on him, and even at the very moment when he calls her by the name Nounoune 'which he had given her as a child, and which he suddenly uttered from the depths of his pleasure like a cry for help', he reveals nothing of himself. Always a malicious impulse reasserts itself (he confesses one day that this streak of malice somehow consoles him) 'as soon as he began to speak, being careful to keep his true self hidden'.

No one has ever plumbed 'those large pupils, whose lustre was enhanced by the pureness of the surrounding whites . . .' to reach down to 'the heart of Chéri, hard and late-burgeoning as an oak bud'.

There is something utterly inhuman about Chéri right from the start. He has already given Léa the feeling that she is as remote from him as she might be from 'a Chinese or a Negro'. An even more revealing sidelight on his character is given us by Edmée, his young wife: 'There are times when he is like a savage. . . . He knows nothing of plants or animals, and at times he even seems not to know anything of humanity. . . .' Edmée begins by loving him for his exceptional beauty, but because she is young and impatient, she is not steadfast enough to wait for an eventual change in him; instead, she gives herself to the first comer, and Chéri is left alone.

A few weeks after his marriage, he does, indeed, return one night to Léa, and for the first time shows such a tender transport of passion that Léa, overwhelmed, realizes that she herself also genuinely loves someone for the first time, and spends the night making plans for a future in which she and Chéri will be indissolubly united. But in the morning, Chéri surprises her studying the railway timetable, 'not yet powdered, with a meagre twist of hair at the back of her head, double-chinned and scrawny-necked'. Gripped by an instinctive horror, he cannot prevent himself betraying, by his horrified pity, that he finds her aged. Léa's interior tumult, her terrible conversion to the idea that from now on she must look upon herself as an old woman, are successive stages which we see her encompass at a single bound, in the disinterestedness and generosity of her heart. She even urges Chéri to hasten off in pursuit of his youth, which has been 'barely curtailed by ageing women...by misdirected mother-love'. 'You've had a taste of youth,' she tells him. 'You know it never satisfies, but one still goes back for more.'

She has also told him: 'I've loved you as if we were both destined to die, you and I, an hour later. Because I was born twenty-four years before you, I was doomed, and I dragged you down with me.' She sees how Chéri, as he departs down the avenue, throws back his head to look at the spring sky, and fills his lungs with air, like a man escaping from prison.

Years go by, and Chéri sees no more of Léa. It does not even occur to him that he might one day want to see her again. The war of 1914–18 passes over him but leaves no scars. He shows bravery in battle, without really knowing why, and comes out of it decorated and richer than before, in the company of men and women who have also grown

rich through the war, and think only of enriching themselves further. But something unexpected gradually
happens to Chéri: money and business interests, eating
and drinking, all the things that have formerly been
sufficient to occupy his time, now begin to lose their
hold on him. And here, if it were not apparent at the
outset that Colette is a novelist pure and simple (in fact,
she never aimed at being anything else), one might well
discern an unexpected foretaste of 'existentialist' changes
of feeling in the behaviour of her character. If we suppose
for a moment that Sartre, after writing *La Nausée*, had
had the idea for *La Fin de Chéri*, one would at once see in
it a masterly, and what we would call 'phenomenological',
analysis of the hero's feeling of nausea when confronted
with existence. One could draw an entire series of parallels
between Chéri and Sartre's hero. For example, Chéri's
indignation at 'those rotters' is of the same kind as
Roquentin's as he surveys the portraits of Bouville's
worthies. It is not merely that they both employ the same
epithet, it is the same scorn that compels them to stigmatize the hypocritical money-making and the bland
insincerity of those who are so certain of being 'in their
rights', in other words, of being backed up by all the
forces of law and order in the country.

One really wonders whether it is Chéri or Roquentin
speaking, in a passage of dialogue like this:

' "Do you really call that a life?"

' "What life?" (asks his mother, who has become direc-
tor of a hospital for war wounded).

' "My life. Yours. Everything. Everything one sees . . .
these fellows . . . this army . . . this peace."

'He stretched his fingers wide apart as if they were
sticky or entangled in overlong hair.' (One notes the use
of adjectives oddly like those typical of existentialism.)

' "What's the matter with you?"

' "The matter is that everyone's rotten . . . present
company not excepted. . . . You have your blankets,
your macaroni and spaghetti, your *légions d'honneur*. You
joke about what's going on in parliament . . . there's the
wounded, the dance halls . . . the American cigars . . . in
short, they're rotten, the lot of them. . . ."

' "That doesn't tell me what you're driving at."

' " . . . I don't really know myself. I just wish people
weren't such rotters all the time . . . or rather, I just wish
I didn't have to notice it."

' "Why do you notice it, then?"

' "Ah, there you are. . . . That's the whole question." '

As we might guess, the question remains unanswered,
for Chéri as much as for Roquentin. Things are simply
what they are, and there is no penetrating their opaque
reality.

'He felt empty and abandoned, filled with yearning for

all that he lacked.' From that point onwards, Chéri is slowly undermined from within. He has not grown mature, it is true, indeed he will never reach maturity, but he can no longer continue to be a solitary unaware of his own solitude. There is only one recourse for him: Léa.

Like a sleep-walker, or rather, like a child who insists that the years have not rolled by, and who dreams of finding intact and unharmed the single lost chance of carefree happiness, and perhaps its own single generous impulse, he rings at Léa's door.

In literature there are few greater achievements than the description of this final encounter. It is a man's whole life that is at stake, although he himself has no clear awareness of the fact. Chéri comes back to Léa like someone who can no longer bear the unending sterility of his own existence, and must return to the place where once, at least for a brief space, he wielded a sort of creative power. . . . He knows perfectly well that he has had nothing to give to Edmée, who is young and beautiful in her own right and can get along quite happily without him. But in the old days, it was something like his own youth that he gave whenever he ran to Léa, and she would look at him with rekindled gaze.

He enters and sees, her back turned towards him, a woman with the neck of an elderly cellist, and thick, vigorous grey hair. Where is Léa? he wonders. 'The grey-

haired woman turned round, and Chéri received the full
impact of her blue eyes.'

' "Ah, good heavens, child, it's you!" '

The same words, almost the same low-pitched laugh,
and the same blue eyes as before, although now they have
grown smaller. But it is no longer the same Léa. 'Her arms
stood out from the armpits like rounded thighs, propped
up on layers of fat, and the long nondescript jacket of her
tailored costume proclaimed a woman who had abdi-
cated, had renounced her femininity . . . acquiring a sort
of sexless dignity.' Nevertheless, Chéri is not too deeply
shocked at first glance, by her cubic bulk. It is only when,
standing at the window, she reveals her features that he
begins 'to implore her with silent entreaties, as he would
have done an armed madman', for it is her face that cuts
him to the quick. If only it were someone else, this
'healthy old woman with sagging jowls and double chin',
with 'her red face, of a rather over-ripe redness, for now
she scorned the use of powder, and laughed to reveal a
mouth full of gold teeth'.

Chéri realizes that he is completely lost. There is
nothing to be done about it. He can no longer strike a
spark from that calm and placid mass; no longer stir up
the secret struggle between them. No one needs him any
longer, and he himself, although formerly he was easily
enough satisfied, only asking that Léa should retain the

semblance of youth needed to kindle his love, can no longer discern in the woman she has become the least charm that might still provide fuel for that love. He is confronted with an insurmountable paradox: his love is intact, and even stronger than ever, since he has achieved self-awareness; but it no longer has an object.

The admirable scene that now unfolds is played out on two levels. Here is Léa who once, long ago, when she gave Chéri back his freedom, watched with horror the breathless old woman who repeated all her movements in the glass, and asked herself what she could have in common with such a crazy creature, here is the same Léa happily exhibiting an old man's joviality, and asking Chéri a few cautious questions about both his business affairs and the state of his digestion; and here is Chéri replying with short, banal phrases, while his double kneels, haggard and imploring, feeling all the blood drain from his heart, silently entreating the shade of the woman he has loved to put on flesh once more, and drive from the room the grotesque but too solid stranger who has taken her place: 'Stop!' he silently implores her, 'Come back again! Throw off your disguise. You must be lurking there somewhere, for it's your voice I hear! Reveal yourself! Arise like a creature reborn, with your hair hennaed only this morning, your face freshly powdered; put on your long stays once more, the blue dress with its delicate jabot, the scent like a meadow that I search for in vain in your new house. . . . Leave all this, and come away to Passy, fresh from a shower, Passy with its dogs and its birds, come to the Avenue Bugeaud where, sure enough, Ernest will be polishing the brass on the front door. . . .'

From that scene onwards to the very end of the book, to the final moment when Chéri, his eyes riveted on the photograph of a Léa in the full bloom of youth, not as he ever knew her but as he overwhelmingly longs to join her now, presses the revolver against his temple, we watch a slow ascent (if one can use such a term for a process of decay) towards the final rejection of life by one who never had any affection for himself, and dies from his failure to acquire self-knowledge and to come to terms with himself.

The fact that this novel has been, and continues to be, a success for the wrong reasons does not matter. By 'the wrong reasons', I mean the swiftness with which all women who feel their own youth threatened have gone on through the years identifying themselves with the character of Léa, and the number of young girls who have exclaimed to Colette: 'We know Chéri, Madame, we have met Chéri!' They have merely been content to follow the superficial outline of the story. But behind that outline there is a whole psychology evoked by

'Chéri', an analysis of a particular fear that achieves a universal validity: the fear liable to strike anyone who sees his beloved growing old before his eyes. Chéri expresses the horror everyone feels at the spectacle of human collapse and decay.

VI

Colette Among Her Contemporaries

Should I not have departed sooner from this earthly realm?

LA NAISSANCE DU JOUR

It must be admitted that, where certain of Colette's characters are concerned, one is sometimes tempted to paraphrase Léon-Paul Fargue's witty summing-up at the end of an article on Proust (whom, for that matter, he admired): 'All the same, it is a pity that he was so infatuated with nonentities, conceited fools and bores.' In the same way, one is tempted to exclaim of Colette: 'What a pity she was so fond of pimps and prostitutes and aimless drifters!' For the fact remains that Colette's achievement consists in involving us in the fate of people whose existence would have left us totally indifferent if we had encountered them in reality, but who fascinate us under her pen.

Why, indeed, did she show such a constant preoccupation with those whom she herself regarded as 'vampires', or, as she sometimes called them, 'barnacles',[1] thereby

[1] *Chambre d'Hôtel.*

stressing the risk one runs in maintaining contact with creatures devoid of substance themselves, and only too happy to feed on the substance of others?

The heroine of *La Vagabonde* has told us how disgusted she felt, after her divorce, with the ultra-intellectual circle in which she had lived and suffered, and how much she needed to limit herself henceforth to 'primitive beings who would scarcely think at all'.

In *Mes Apprentissages*, Colette tells us that she never sought out those 'whom other men call great', for she was too saddened that 'their fame made them pale shadows, anxious to fit into a mould, to be consistent with themselves above all. . . .'[1] She preferred the casual encounter, the passing stranger, those whom she refers to as 'savoury and obscure'. . . . People such as these aroused in her a positive passion of curiosity. For 'just as the finest dishes do not prevent a sudden longing for saveloys, no more can a sensitive and tested friendship deprive one of a taste for what is new and questionable'.

It is chiefly to matters concerning love that Colette applies this curiosity. But since the normal offers no spring-board to the imagination, she prefers to go roam-

[1] It should be noted, however, that Colette, with her unrivalled gift as a portraitist, brings to life in an extraordinary way the appearance and behaviour of certain of her contemporaries, whether it be Proust, Renée Vivien or Barthou, or her dearest friends, Cocteau, Marguerite Moreno, Germaine Beaumont, Hélène Morhange.

ing well off the orthodox path. At the outset Claudine exclaims: 'I want to get to know women who live by their charms, so long as they are gay and temperamental, or even melancholy and quiet, as are many courtesans.' It is a plan of action that Colette fulfils by dwelling on Madame Peloux and her friends, Léa's 'pals', and those far-sighted women trading on their charms who fill the main roles in *Gigi*. She also shows a marked interest in the world of perverts, to whom she devotes several pages of carefully detailed analysis far removed from the frivolous tone of her early novels. It was through a negro secretary of Willy's that Colette was led into close contact with homosexual circles. 'Formerly', she tells us, 'the only atmosphere I enjoyed, the only atmosphere I called "pure", was that from which women were excluded.' It is also in this sphere that we can observe the play of what one might call Colette's 'feeling for categories'. Phrases such as 'we, as women', or 'men, for their part', or 'women like that with an illicit love-life', or 'when it comes to pederasts', show us how she tended to reduce human beings to a common denominator.[1] In these particular matters, she differs essentially from

---

[1] Colette shows us just how subtle her art can be, however, the moment she leaves formulas aside and turns to deal with the particular, in her moving account of the loves of the two old maids of Llangollen, who died three hundred years ago.

Proust. In *Les jeunes filles en fleurs*, it is only gradually that we come to understand the fundamental ambiguity concealed beneath the tomboyish caprices of 'the little band'; it is only after a rigorous analysis of these psychological characteristics that Proust finally suggests to us what Albertine's perversion must be, but by then there is no risk of diminishing her character. In Colette's case, on the contrary, her characters are conceived as generalizations from the start, and remain within the general, so that their human complexity gradually dwindles away. Her abnormal characters have no greater psychological resources than her light-o'-loves or her middle-class protagonists. We often find ourselves confronted with individuals who lack a sufficiently rich inner life to express themselves in the first person, and are thus reduced to being simply the 'third person' – 'the person one talks about', as Gide said. It is worth noting, besides, what Colette herself confides to us about her methods of eavesdropping on life. 'It is a sort of calculated licence. . . . And then one must still translate, or in other words, raise to its secret significance, a litany of dull and lifeless words.'

By comparison with those faithfully transcribed lifeless conversations,[1] the *lingua franca* of the music-hall artists

[1] cf., for example, the remarks of the two innkeepers in *Bella Vista*, or of the characters in *Rendez-vous*.

comes as a refreshment to the spirit. Furthermore, it is in
L'Envers du Music-Hall, with its struggling throng of half-
starved humanity, that we feel the pulse of Colette's
warm and watchful compassion for her neighbour. From
poor Gonzalès, 'light as a dry leaf', with 'the macabre
choreographic grace of a young dancing skeleton', who
trembles with cold in an overcoat 'yellowed by the suns
and rains of the preceding years', to the aged ballet-dancer
who, in spite of her bronchitis, 'rehearses with forty
cupping-glasses on her back and runs to the lavatory with
her coughing fit' to avoid being replaced on the spot, she
gives us an admirable impression of the pride-in-adversity
of those whom she calls 'my glittering and impoverished
brothers', those who, despite sickness and hunger, cling
fiercely and even unto death to the title of 'artiste'. But
apart from these clumsy avowals, in which at least one
finds a conviction of being 'dedicated' to something
higher than the individual, the pages devoted to the
human species all too often prove disappointing.

✱　　✱　　✱

> *It is not by being the first to see something new, but
> rather by seeing as if they were new those things that
> everyone knows and is familiar with, that truly
> original minds distinguish themselves.*
>
> NIETZSCHE

If Colette's universe provides no ground for genuine
human contacts, it is very much *the* point of contact with

the animal and vegetable world. It is only here that we may encounter the purest and most all-embracing form of communion.

'My enchanted realm cannot exist without animals'; and it is, in fact, by a wave of the enchanter's wand that she brings the animal to life before us. As for the suspicion with which she regards the human animal, Colette even extends it to the monkey as well: 'The eyes are too beautiful, they hold me at a distance. I am forever on my guard against the human feeling that lurks there, only half-hidden, like a tear.' It is the only slur she casts on our 'lower brothers'. From the grasshopper 'with equine head' to the tawny owl 'with Mary Stuart ruff', from the little sow rooting up truffles at dawn, 'rose-pink under her sparse bristles, naked in the icy dew', to the Brazilian squirrel which 'combs itself with its ten fingers like a Romantic poet and arches over its back a tail like a question mark', there are few animals that cannot claim a large place in this bestiary compiled with such tender understanding.

'I am used to expecting miracles,' she tells us in *Prisons et Paradis*. Miracles do, in fact, constantly occur; wherever she goes, something happens. She sets off to look for lily-of-the-valley in the forest of Rambouillet, and her hand discovers at ground level a warm little pheasant sitting on her nest. She goes for a walk on a spring morn-

ing, with a dog that is losing its winter coat by the handful; and two pairs of tomtits follow her, threatening to
pluck the dog bare 'in order to furnish their nests'. She
goes wine-harvesting, and discovers 'in a many-layered
skirt of leaves' a large green lizard, which she at once
captures in her cupped hands; a handsome quarry, she tells
us, 'with close-meshed scales and long fingers that tried
to loosen my grip, with a majestic green tail, a blue patch
on each temple, and a small gladiolus-purple throat'.

Dialogues de Bêtes takes the form of a series of pungent
comments exchanged by a dog and a cat, in a manner not
far removed from human conversation, but I find even
more admirable the reflections of Colette herself, as a
great animal-lover, in *La Paix chez les Bêtes* and *Prisons
et Paradis*.

With Colette, a love for animals goes hand in hand
with a desire to tame, in other words, a desire to solicit
and win a confidence she knows herself worthy to share.
She has already told us of those instances when she has
encountered a strange child while out for a walk, and
seen him waver under her scrutiny as if he could not help
confiding his secret to her,[1] and in the same way, an
animal has only to see her to recognize and pay homage
to her superior quality.

[1] To understand another being, she tells us, is to bring that person
under our own domination, to weaken him.

For instance, she goes into a kitchen where a snake has been seen: at once, the snake has no thought for anyone else, and rears up to 'stare her in the face'. 'Like the cat, the horse and the dog, the snake recognizes and interrogates the window of the eye. It seeks a response, it understands.' The entire description is admirable: 'When I go to grasp the snake by its delicate neck, it eludes me, and in vexation inscribes a five, a five and a nought, or else an S, an O, a W, on the oilcoth, fixing me in the eye with its own small golden eyes. In the end, I hold out a stick to it, which it feels, accepts and transforms into a caduceus; then I carry the whole lot out into the garden. But there, it is overcome with nostalgia, leaps up the two steps at a run, if I can use that expression, and climbs back on to the table. How strange its swiftness seems!... The front half of its body darts forward, seems to spring out of itself, leaping into self-created life, while the latter half still waits to move forward and join it....'[1]

As for the wild beasts, we know how strongly Colette was drawn to them. If she never actually went into a lion's cage, she certainly once entered a cage where two leopards were fighting 'like two hostile storm-clouds... thundering down like an avalanche of snow....' 'A May meadow is not more strewn with flowers,' she says of their markings, 'black corollas clustered thickly

[1] *Journal à Rebours.*

on a pale field, flowers with four, three and two petals. . . .'[1]

Colette certainly spared no effort to penetrate to the heart of the wild animal. 'Eyes with their far-off dumb appeal, efforts of the animal to overcome the inviolability it has not sought, direct yourselves towards me once more: I have always come half-way to meet you.'

Since it played such a particular role in her life, we must make special mention of the cat. From childhood on, when her mother called her by the pet name of 'Minet Chéri' ('Darling Kitten'), the cat was her emblem, and she herself has told us how 'poignant and necessary' she always found the feline atmosphere. They are linked by all sorts of affinities. It is to the cat that Colette owes the gift of 'maintaining long silences', as well as that capacity for hiding one's feelings which, she tells us, is the cat's supreme source of fascination. She even goes so far as to say: 'For a woman as for a cat, deceit becomes the first adornment of love.' In *Les Vrilles de la Vigne*, she tells us: 'One can hardly fail to be enriched by living in the company of a cat. It is surely by design that for half a century past, I have sought such company. I never had to look far: it was there, under my feet. Lost cats and farmyard cats, hunters and hunted by turn, gaunt with insomnia, library cats with ink in their veins, the well-fed cats of

[1] *Prison et Paradis.*

dairies and butchers' shops squatting immovable on the
tiles, the wheezing cats of poor households, swollen with
lights: blessed despot-cats who ... hold me in your thrall.'

It is therefore not surprising that the only deliberately
lyrical phrases in her work, an invocation to love, should
be uttered by a cat. Here are the words of the tempter
tomcat, as his complaint comes to the ears of the tabby,
Nonoche:

'Come! ... If you do not come you shall rest no more.
... Reflect that every hour that follows will be the same
as this, filled with my voice, winged with my desire. ...
Come! ...

'You know, you know full well, that I can persist in my
lamentations for nights on end, that I will stop drinking
and stop eating, for desire is enough to keep me alive and
I fortify myself with love! ... Come! ...

'You do not know my face, and little that matters! I
tell you with pride who I am: I am the lean Tom tattered
by ten summers, hardened by ten winters. I limp with
one paw in memory of an old wound, my scarred nostrils
grimace, and my one remaining ear is ragged from the
teeth of my rivals.

'I have slept so long on the hard ground that the earth
has given me its very colour. I have prowled so far and
wide that my calloused pads resound on the track like the
hooves of the roe-deer. I walk with a wolfish gait, hind-

quarters low to the ground, followed by an almost hairless stump of tail. . . . My lean flanks cleave together and my skin ripples round the hard muscles, trained to abduction and rape. . . . And all that ugliness sets me in the image of Love! Come! . . . When I appear before your eyes, you will recognize nothing of me but Love!

'My teeth will force your arching neck into submission, I will sully your robe, I will inflict upon you as many bites as caresses, I will annihilate in you all recollection of your home, and for days and nights, you will be my savage and clamorous companion . . . until that darker hour when you will find yourself once more alone, for I shall mysteriously have fled, tired of you and summoned by her whom I do not know, whom I have not yet possessed. . . . And then, you will creep back to your retreat, famished, humble, mud-bespattered, your eyes pale, your spine sagging as if already weighed down by the fruit of your womb, and take refuge in a long slumber twitching with dreams in which our love is once more resurrected. . . . Come! . . .'[1]

This savage appeal, this recitative so packed with hidden meanings with its extraordinary suggestive power to convey a reality that seems to be unfolding before our eyes, takes us to the very heart of Colette's magic – the magic of her style.

[1] *Les Vrilles de la Vigne.*

VII

Colette as a Stylist

*French is certainly a difficult language. One has been
writing for a bare forty-five years when that fact
begins to dawn on one.*

JOURNAL À REBOURS

AN appearance of the liveliest spontaneity, allied to the
most meticulous feeling for the rhythm and weight of the
words: that is the chief characteristic of Colette's style.
Her innate gift for music has often been invoked in order
to explain the melodic structure of her sentences, but
musical intuition alone cannot be made to account for her
unrivalled and perpetually renewed power to find the
right word. One also often hears it said that Colette's
art is the triumph of an extraordinary naturalism, and at
least as far as method is concerned, she is said to have
affinities with Jules Renard and Zola. But there is an
essential difference. Colette did not 'choose' the particular form in which she was to express herself: it was
imposed on her, to the exclusion of all others, by her very
nature; and thus, one cannot talk of 'method' in her case.
In spite of appearances, what we find in her work is not

[136]

merely a description, but a re-creation of nature, to which the term 'naturalist' cannot properly be applied. What tends to confuse matters is that, at first sight, the whole of Colette's work appears to conform to the definition laid down by Mallarmé for the exponents of naturalism: 'After all, what are these people doing?' he asked. 'They weave their narration round things we already know. They discover the Trocadero, dance-halls, Japan. What I myself contribute to literature is the fact that I do not set myself before a scene and say: what is it? while I try to describe it as best I can, but that I say: what does it mean?'

The quest for finality, for a definitive description, is not at all Colette's intention. She is perfectly ready to content herself with the mere presence of reality, without trying to elicit any response from it. But she is not content just to describe it, instead she sets out to explore it, virtually to re-create it. That is why, without specifically aiming to do so, Colette is able to satisfy a certain metaphysical need in us. She provides a perfect illustration of Valéry's formula: 'The artist creates that which he unveils'. In short, reality is certainly present in things, but it must be extracted from them, prised free from the matrix which holds it captive.

Extraction and incantation are, for Colette, two different modes of approach to the real. The slightest observed phenomenon is enough to bring this power into opera-tion. As often as not, she proceeds by simple analogy, as when she speaks of the 'toad with its gullet full of pearls', or of 'the silken sound, as of a fan opened and shut, of a pigeon on the wing', of 'the damp whispering of a handful of shrimps' or of 'sulky May, shedding her harness of roses under the showers', but in every case the kernel of reality is stripped of its husk. We are thus confronted at the outset by a strange paradox: the mind instantly recognizes the inevitable truth of these images, and yet, without Colette, they would have remained hidden from us.

'If you would know the infinite, study the finite from every aspect,' Goethe tells us. The art of Colette completely explores and exhausts the finite, without ever entering upon the infinite. Nevertheless, a 'finite' such as hers holds in store all the surprises of the most fabulous discoveries. We may, for example, through her description of it, join her in a first ascent in a balloon. 'I had never experienced the fantastic sensation of floating,' she tells us, 'until that day when I climbed over the rim of a small square basket hanging beneath an impatient yellow planet, and crossed the Seine.' One of the last sounds the aeronaut caught as she leaned from the basket was 'the rippling hiss of sand puncturing the water. . . . After that, the sphere leapt into the air with such speed it was like falling upwards. It soared ever deeper into the sky, carving a place for itself in the very heart of the silence, until at last the wind took it under its wing.' We share her sensation of becoming 'a bubble, an irresponsible and wandering seed'. We, too, join in the hazards of the voyage. 'Someone threw a handful of petals overboard, which melted away as if drunk by the air. "That's because we're still rising," said a voice. Later in the day, another released handful of butterflies seemed to hang in motionless suspense, as if drawn against a ceiling that skimmed past over our heads. "Ah, now we're going down." '[1]

As for the adventure of motherhood, few women have given us a more vivid account than Colette of '... that absorbed study of a new arrival, who has entered the house without coming in from outside....'

'... Did I put enough love into that contemplation?' she goes on. 'I dare not say so for certain. I did indeed have the habit – I have it still – of wonderment. I exerted it on the collection of miracles that is a new-born baby. Nails as transparent as the curved carapace of the rosy shrimp, the soles of the feet that come to us without touching the earth.... The fine down of eyelashes, lowered on the cheek, dividing terrestrial landscapes and the blue dream of the eye.... The tiny sign of sex like a barely incised almond, bivalve neatly closed lip to lip....'[2]

[1] *L'Etoile Vesper.*   [2] *A portée de la main.*

[139]

We find another example in the simple description Colette gives us of the bulldog bitch, Fossette, attacking dogs bigger than herself in the street. 'With a genius for mime, she terrorizes them, twisting her Japanese dragon's mask into convulsions, pulling an abominable grimace that sets her eyes starting out of her head, curling back her lips to show, in the blood-red lining, a number of white fangs sticking out at all angles, like the stakes of a palissade tilted over by the wind.'[1]

Such descriptions as these enrich our perception of the visible world. The banal and the extraordinary are, in fact, the twin aspects of reality. Our eyes soon lose their virgin freshness of outlook, and no longer have power to confront us with anything but the mournful aspect of banality. Colette utilizes all that we waste in our daily lives. But the method she uses is what we might call 'stripping the banal from reality'. Orpheus transformed the savage beasts into tame companions. Colette uses a contrary art to change the most time-worn aspects of daily life into something new and strange. When we suddenly discover this strange new reality, we find it difficult to believe that it has been constructed from nothing more than our precious everyday reality.

$$\star \qquad \star \qquad \star$$

[1] *La Vagabonde.*

There is one fact that one does not notice at first, and which may well strike the reader as an irreverent, almost a sacriligeous, observation: Colette has no style! But, it will be objected, what about those fixed and irrevocable phrases, not a word of which can be displaced without upsetting their perfect harmony, surely they express a style? Yet these are not a matter of style, for the simple reason that Colette's genius springs from the very source of reality, hers is a direct contact, the shortest path that can be traversed to reach the heart of the real. She needs no intermediary to transmit her subject to us, and hence, no style, since style is precisely that which contains the subject.

One can always imitate a style. Reality alone is inimitable, and that is why one cannot make a pastiche of Colette without actually copying the outline of her phrases in one way or another, thereby making it clear that one is trying to imitate her. In the normal way, style is something we can lift from an author, the means by which we come to know him, and the spur with which another author can surreptitously set his own inspiration in motion. But one cannot lift a style from Colette, since the envelope, the intermediary, has disappeared, and one is dealing only with the phenomenon in its pure state.

For example, how, after her, is one to speak of a dying rose, or convey one's feelings at that delicate mortality: 'We all shudder when a rose, disintegrating in a warm room, abandons one of its shell-shaped petals, sends it sailing down to its own reflection on a smooth marble surface. The sound of its fall, very low but distinct, is like a syllable of silence and enough to move a poet.'[1] Or here is the peony at its final moment: 'The peony sheds its bloom all at once, and lets fall round the base of the vase a circle of petals.'

Colette creates a truth at once obvious and definitive, which turns back upon itself in the form of a spiral. 'I am by nature drawn to the curve,' she tells us. Her imagery engenders microcosms, within whose narrow compass the reader finds himself held by sheer delight, moved by the same nostalgia for perfection in miniature which once filled his childhood with tremulous longings to enter the doll's house or the music box; she reveals to us an absolute that is always within our reach, that we can always turn to.

Confronted by such an achievement, our reason may well give up the task of trying to explain it. That which is left incomplete has its own power, its own virtue to provoke fresh growth. It has been said that there can be no life except in the heart of imperfection (Saint Augustine). This perhaps explains the inertia with which our mind seems to be afflicted when it is confronted with anything complete and perfect in itself. Perfection refers to nothing

[1] *Flore et Pomone.*

but itself, and provides no impulse to go beyond it. By taking this argument to the extreme, one might say the same of both Colette's and the so-called classical style. To the question raised by the very perfection of the finest verses of Racine, that perfection itself can alone give answer. There is a rigorous consonance between the situation posed in these two lines and the strict economy with which it is resolved:

> *Et Phèdre, au labyrinthe, avec vous descendue*
> *Se serait, avec vous, retrouvée ou perdue.*

The same could be said of certain verses of La Fontaine, or of certain of La Bruyère's aphorisms that everyone knows. Perfection absolves us of the need to invent: we are not asked to erect our own edifice on certain bases presented to our imagination. We have been given a golden key with which we are able to enter the completed house. Powerless and dazed, we can do no more than wait for the hour to strike. Nothing is expected of us. Our collaboration is not needed.

But perhaps it is by the approach, the insinuation of a truth hinted at but never stated, that a literary work of art arouses us to an awareness of our own creative potentialities. There is that remark of Alain's, for example: 'Magic is the spirit that lurks in material things.' At once our attention is aroused, echoes awaken within us, unexpected depths are revealed: we had not known how rich we were.

When Rimbaud exclaims –

> *Le bonheur:*
> *Sa dent douce à la mort*
> *M'avertissait au chant du coq*
> *Alleluia! dans les plus sombres villes . . .*

here certainly is the ineffable hint of a truth that is not formulated. Or when Claudel, speaking of the death of Dona Prouhèze, declares:

> *Elle n'est pas si morte que ce ciel autour de nous et cette*
> *mer sous nos pieds ne soient encore plus éternels!*

the truth suggested by these opposing statements remains unexpressed; in other words, it is still at liberty, free to set us off in pursuit, in the hope of bringing it down at our feet, still warm, with a well-aimed shaft of secret understanding.

It must not be thought that it is because, in this case, I am no longer dealing with images but with ideas that perfection is no longer held captive. For what could be more 'thought out', and yet still remain so shut-in, than this further passage from Colette, which I have chosen at random, dealing with inner renunciation: 'What is the use? Any form of renunciation brings its own moment of unavowable pleasure, a pleasure experienced with arms hanging limp and head thrown back, as if in sensual enjoyment.'[1]

If, in the long run, we feel simultaneously so poor and so rich in the presence of Colette, that is because she presents us with a blinding reality that our mind immediately grasps, and yet one which, without her, would have remained hidden from us. We are told that profundity and obscurity go together, and that clarity manifests itself just beneath the surface. With Colette, the most profound truth and the most obvious truth are revealed simultaneously: therein lies the paradoxical nature of her achievement. Cocteau has said: 'The poet liberates from the dark,' meaning that it is his mission to express the obscure truth of which he makes himself the bearer. Colette, for her part, liberates from the light, which is why she is something very different from a poet. Not only does she invoke reality by incantation, she also shows us that reality is not self-sufficient, but that it has no ties with us unless we succeed in bringing it under our sway. It is not by chance that in ancient times, certain peoples made it a rule that God must never be invoked by name. To name something accurately was, and still is, a way of bringing it under one's power. Colette teaches us that it is by the appropriate word that one really gains possession

[1] *Journal à Rebours.*

of things. Whenever, seeing a particular movement of the sea or the clouds, the unfurling of a wing or a flag, the behaviour of an animal in a garden, we experience a sense of helplessness at the useless profusion with which things thrust themselves upon us, since we are powerless to take possession of them by an incantatory word, we can but turn – even though irked by our failure to conquer the difficulty for ourselves, and seeking, as it were, a reward we have not deserved – to Colette who makes things more tangible to us than our own senses, to Colette who will always endure first and foremost as a giver of names.

VIII

The Art of Growing Old

PORTRAIT OF A STOIC

Guided by the same hand, pen and needle, the habit of work and the wise desire to work no more, come together, separate, are reconciled once more. . . . Try to run in harness, my slow chargers: already I can see the end of the road.

L'ETOILE VESPER

IN Colette's life, there are two aspects of major significance: sickness and old age. For, even more vividly than an art of living, what she gives us is an art of growing old.

The longer the road a person has had to travel before reaching the final state of resignation, the greater one's admiration. We certainly have every reason to admire Colette when we see how far she had to travel from her childhood, from that early period when she would 'shy' like an animal at the smell of sickness or old age, through the years of her maturity when she tells us she still 'stopped her nostrils' because sickness and old age would soon 'have her in their grip', to that final period when, immobilized by a painful arthritis, she was still able to transmute so much zest for life into a stoicism masked by serene good humour.[1]

It is in *La Naissance du Jour*, with its premonitory evocation of Colette's later renunciation of love, which takes us on to the downward slope of life, that all the elements of the drama are finally established. It is a woman of over fifty who speaks to us from these pages, in which all that is lost is secretly weighed against all that can be considered as won. The days are over, Colette tells us, when the woman could appear as a symbol of abundance, pouring out her riches without limit in an

[1] In *Les Vrilles de la Vigne*, written when she was thirty-three, there appears this passage, which foreshadows the resigned mood of her last years: 'I am astonished to discover that I have aged even as I was dreaming. . . . On the face before me now, I could with feeling paint in once more the features of a little girl freckled by the sun . . . mobile cheeks descending to a pointed chin, darting eyebrows quick to come together, a mouth sly at the corners, belying the artlessness of the short upper lip. . . . Alas, the moment is soon gone. . . . The sombre waters of the mirror hold only my present image . . . with the faint lines, as of finger-nail markings, drawn delicately across the eyelids, at the corners of the lips, between the stubborn eyebrows. . . . An image neither smiling nor sad, which murmurs for my ear alone: "You must grow old. Do not weep, do not clasp your hands in supplication, do not rebel: you must grow old. Repeat those words to yourself, not as a cry of despair, but as if to remind yourself of a journey that must be made. . . . Already you are beginning to leave your life behind, do not forget it, you must grow old!" ' We find this same sharp regret for passing youth expressed just as intensely by Madame de Noailles, but shot through with a despair, impregnated with a pathos, that Colette would not have allowed herself.

'egoistic frenzy', exclaiming to the man whose love she has gratified: 'Take! Don't think of refusing, unless you want me to die of overabundance!' Now the time has come when 'a woman has nothing to do but to enrich herself.' And for the first time, Colette glimpses the feeling of liberation that comes to a passionate nature once the heart and senses have found peace.

'One of the great commonplaces of existence – love – is withdrawing from my life.... It seems to me that a great new relationship is beginning between man and myself. ... Man, my friend, shall we breathe in harmony? I have always loved your company. Now the look you hold for me is so gentle. You see emerging, from a discarded confusion of feminine tackle, that yet clings heavily as seaweed, a shipwrecked survivor ... you see your sister, your comrade, emerging: a woman escaping from the age of her womanhood.... Let us stay together: there is no longer any reason now why you should leave me ever.'[1]

The age of friendship is at last beginning. The age, too, when one can look back and tell oneself that, all things considered, one has proved one's courage. 'No one did me mortal hurt in my past. Suffering? Yes, I had suffering in plenty. But is that such a grave matter?... I begin to doubt it.' And speaking of her heart: 'How strongly it

[1] *La Naissance du Jour.*

beat, how strongly it fought ! . . . There now, heart, beat
gently. . . . It is time to rest ! You scorned to seek happiness, let us take credit for that. . . . We were never in any
danger . . . of settling down to live happily in common-
place contentment.'[1] We have already seen this sovereign
disdain for happiness foreshadowed in the young Colette
of twenty when, observing that before her unfortunate
marriage to Willy her life had been nothing but roses, she
added: 'But what should I have done with a life that went
on being nothing but roses?' She had laid down her own
path, and to that she remained unswervingly constant;
and now we can clearly perceive the lines on which her
personality was to assume its final form.

La Naissance du Jour evokes that dawning clarity that
awaits the wise once they have penetrated the obscuring
veil of the senses. But however lucidly one might have
expected such a being, made to achieve constant victories
of will, to conduct the struggle for self-domination, one
could not have foreseen what her reaction would be to
physical suffering and the slow ebbing away of vitality.

After having set the highest value on the claims of the
flesh, Colette's triumph consists precisely in a renunciation
of the flesh. Natures more ascetically inclined, people to
all appearances better spiritually prepared, provide us
every day with instances of disillusionment when their

[1] *La Naissance du Jour.*

[150]

final hour comes. Yet in the works that followed *La Naissance du Jour*, scarcely any modification can be detected in Colette's vision. Before her still stretched almost the entire period of her major novels, to the writing of which she was to devote fifteen years. But each time that a personal interlude, such as the *Journal à Rebours* or *Paris de ma fenêtre*, appears in the larger canvas of her imaginative work, we see that her inner landscape has remained the same.[1] There are, indeed, certain phrases in which her celebrated capacity for generalization comes into play – an additional form of modesty as it were – as when she remarks that 'middle-aged women should not ...show themselves before the morning toilet', or, addressing a young woman friend, refers to 'women of your generation', etc.: these merely tell us that Colette herself considered she had now gained a certain eminence from which she was better able to follow the working out of a process that no longer concerned her. But with *L'Etoile Vesper* and *Le Fanal Bleu* the evolutionary process is complete. The woman who speaks to us is no longer one whose body leads her wherever she desires and who feels the whole universe within her reach, but a woman

---

[1] I have not mentioned in this context *Mes Apprentissages*, which nevertheless belongs to the same period. But although dated 1936, this book looks back deliberately to Colette's youth, and deals with events that had occurred nearly forty years earlier.

suffering from ill-health and more often than not bed-ridden. Once again, someone has come to 'cut Cybele's tresses', and this time it is old age and sickness, which she so much hated. Here is a woman of over seventy, and at the very end, of nearly eighty, talking to us, and one who has less and less respite from pain. What can we expect to hear from one who was always so fiercely on the side of life, from one who formerly confessed herself incapable of feeling the slightest regret at the death of a flower: 'The images and symbols of a gracious death are not at all to my taste. . . . The corolla's extinction leaves me unmoved. But I am filled with exaltation by the flower that is just beginning its cycle. . . . What is the majesty of the final moment compared with the hesitant departures, and the confusions of the dawn?'[1] What can she tell us when, holding no belief, she could not attribute to suffering the least redemptive value? Filled with a sheer love of being alive even now, she remarks: 'Fortunately, my suffering is of that sort that hopes for relief, but does not foresee life coming to an end.' Here we see once more the enduring elements in her personality: the courage and the will to mastery over the self that were always hers, beneath a certain appearance of self-indulgence and the search for pleasurable sensation. But we have already seen this acceptance of pain, the recognition of the place it has a

[1] *Flore et Pomone.*

right to in a person's life, on the same footing as any other vital manifestation, in Colette's remark thirty years earlier, speaking of the anguish of unrequited love: 'How terrible it is each time the pain comes back! . . . But a worse thing can happen. . . . There comes the moment when your suffering will almost have ceased . . . when you will have lost that fine, passionate, vibrant and tyrannical despair.'[1]

Even in old age, she still had sufficient resources to dread that diminution of ardour that, for her, was the other name for serenity. She wondered if she had not broken away too easily from those sufferings that properly belong not only to youth, but to all whose lives span the full range of their potentialities. Thus she congratulated herself on having preserved at least that source of all ardour: her femininity. 'Even till jealous death, even crowned with white hair, love clings to the inestimable pain of loving.' Years before, she had made one of her heroines remark that a woman must be old indeed when she could bear to dispense with a spectator for her life. For more than twenty years, Colette herself did indeed have close to her, as close to her as her own shadow, one who was more than a spectator, one whose constant care it was, by a thousand attentions, to keep her in contact with the healthy outside world.

[1] *Les Vrilles de la Vigne.*

'What a strange thing it is, a life from which every touch of malice gradually drains away!' Colette exclaims. 'Not to tell harmless lies any more, not to speak ill of anyone.' We can sense that she is on the brink of being astonished by her own radical transformation, she who used to say that 'lying is a lover's finest adornment'. The desire to please never left her, and it continued to be her rule that she must always look her best, whatever her inner mood and her more and more weakened physical state. She continued therefore to make herself up with care, to laugh and crack a joke, after the murmur of pain when the doctors came to her bedside, or rather, as she puts it, 'to the side of the divan which gives me space to suffer and work, the divan-raft on which, for so many years, I have been floating'.

Above all, it would be quite wrong to think of her as sad, in her room looking on to the tranquil garden of the Palais Royal, with swallows and children's cries darting through the air. She loved that prospect of identical façades, with their regularly-spaced fluted pilasters. In that quarter of Paris, quiet as a country retreat, she found the same inspiration as in her old village. It was here that, from now on, she found most of her subjects. 'That noise . . . did you hear it? A discreet murmur of something giving way. . . . It's nothing', she tells us, 'it's the Palais Royal crumbling. Don't worry about it any more than we do who live here.'[1] 'We are all held here by a spell,' she adds, 'a spell preserving at the centre of Paris all that sinks and that endures, all that succumbs and stands firm.' In this apartment where she lived for ten years, she tells us, 'the vertical bends, the horizontal sags like a hammock, the woodwork of the windows goes to powder like old coffee grounds'. But Colette proclaims herself 'stubbornly content with her window', from which she can look down at the passers-by and at life as if from a ship's poop, 'entrenched in her Palais Royal like a winkle in its shell'. On the walls all round her hang 'flowered tapestry, floral still-life paintings, Second Empire photographs, succulent little canvases by her painter friends', but no portraits, since, Colette tells us, she had always 'feared the baleful human countenance in portrait form, the excess of human life that clings to the canvas'. On the bookshelves, a few framed colour-plates from a large folio on pomology, and in glass cases, her entire collection of butterflies. On the mantelpiece, the glass paperweights that fascinated her by their imprisoned spirals round which the light spins and is held captive. Red curtains framed the window where, once the fine weather came, she would have the head of the bed drawn up, so as to have an illusion of sleeping out of doors. And on its mobile pedestal, the shaded lamp, the *fanal bleu*,

[1] *Mélanges.*

[155]

stood by, the symbol, perhaps, for a ship setting sail into the night.

It was from this divan-raft that she charted the course of her last years, those years she spoke of with a touch of bitter irony as 'so heavily laden with honours and maladies'. It was there that she continued to write, not knowing at first, she tells us, whether these pages accumulated at random would ever be published, and yet finding, at the end of the year, that they made up a new book. It was there that she continued to hunt down each word as if it were an elusive prey. But she had acquired the habit of never recoiling from that task. Does she not say, in *Belles Saisons*: 'For me, a holiday means going to work somewhere else'?

Her work was a constant appeal to memory, a process of retracing her steps down all the meanders of a long road. Montaigne had said: 'The years can draw me, if they will, but it is always backwards; so long as my eyes can still perceive the fine season that has gone, I keep turning to glance back at it.' In the same way, Colette kept her eyes fixed on 'the fine season that has gone'.

She herself thought it an excellent thing that she lacked imagination. 'What would have happened if I had roamed after straying nights and dreams? . . . For sixty years I have scoured my own countryside, to winnow one more harvest, to find one more chicken or cat, one more twilight or devoted flower, one further savour.' So she continued to work, without notes or plan. Colette has told us her method: 'I set off, I take to some path I once knew, and fall into my old stride.' Talking of herself in every context and of everything in relation to herself, it was surely, in a sense, her own version of Montaigne's Essays that she was writing. 'To select, to note down the remarkable, to keep the unusual and discard the banal, that is not my way,' she tells us, 'since most of the time it is the ordinary that pricks and stimulates me.'[1] It is by applying her curiosity effectively to the smallest trifles that she has such a tonic effect and gives her readers such a zest for life, like the 'small glass of orange wine' that she recommended to those who were run down in health, or on days of winter cold and mist.

This constant pursuit of fruitful memory, she assures us, was 'a sport and a challenge'. Yet surely it was time now for her to abandon herself to that taste for idleness she had never been able to indulge? Immediately, Colette compares herself to the bay mare her brother Achille once had, and which, harnessed night and day, valiantly trod the roads in fair weather and foul alike. There was always talk of putting the old mare out to grass, but somehow, by force of necessity, she was always back pulling the cart again. I, too, declares Colette, 'I should have stayed

[1] *Le Fanal Bleu.*

longer in the shafts, still lively, still answering the call of
the road. An accident and its consequences have circum-
scribed my lot. . . . All that is needed now is resignation
. . . and a harmonious accord between past and present.'[1]
One feels sure she achieved that harmony. The past
became her chosen sphere, even at night, during those
bouts of insomnia that finally she welcomed and deliberately sought. The present was devoted to a close observation of all that passed before her eyes, and to 'the
manual occupation that introduces a steady rhythm into
the beating of the heart and the movement of one's
thoughts'. Unable now to indulge in gardening or the
various odd jobs at which she had once excelled, the
occupation she chose was tapestry-work. 'Having for
half a century written in black on white, I have now for
nearly ten years been writing with colours on canvas,'
Colette tells us. 'The needle tows its woollen tail along.
. . . My memoirs are being written in blue verdure, in
pink lilacs, in multi-coloured camomile.'[1] Elsewhere she
remarks: 'My woman friends say it amuses me, my truest
friend knows it gives me rest.'

There are occasional moments of revolt: 'I've had
enough ! . . . I want the use of my leg ! A miracle,
heavens above ! It's high time !' But Colette does not

[1] *L'Etoile Vesper.*

seem to have attached any great importance to these, and life went by in a mood of perfect serenity. 'The days not too short, but passing swiftly,' she tells us. And the way in which she relates the small events of each day might well be regarded as her moral testament – although she herself had no such aim, and would have refused to employ such a term (but then it is a common enough thing for a writer to be mistaken about the true nature of his work). Thus, it is in her two last works that we must doubtless look for that 'major theme', that 'general pattern' whose absence one of her friends deplored in her work as a whole, since he felt that such a pattern would have provided her work with 'something like a religion, with dignity, with inspiration'. But illness and suffering slowly and secretly instil in her a new nobility of outlook. Her heart is untainted by envy or bitterness. 'I admire, I rejoice. . . . I brush against and acclaim all these sound-limbed people. Oh! you must not think I am jealous or sad, do me the honour at least of believing that I know how to value what remains to me, to bear gaily with what would once have seemed so heavy a burden, to extract from the infirmity that furrows and divides my being a trace of . . . yes, of nobility. I hesitate, I weigh and examine such a word: what if it were too big for me?' And a little further on: 'I laugh inwardly when very kind people venture the word "asceticism" to fit my case, as if it were some sort of rank. Do people imagine it is easy to escape from asceticism?'[1]

No doubt we are all condemned more or less to asceticism when we reach old age: but surely no one could reach that state in a more open-hearted and generous spirit.

Colette puts to the test the truth that so many people fail to reach: 'The freedom of those who are bound is vast and secret.' We are far removed here from the disenchanted reflection of another woman of genius, Madame de Staël, who considered that a woman was finished the moment she ceased to be 'the first thought in a man's head'. Madame de Staël has a fine and tragic phrase: 'Fame is the brilliant mourning of happiness,' but it is not one we can ever imagine coming from the lips of Colette. In the first place, because she was never greedy for fame; secondly, because she learned at an early age to dispense with happiness; and finally, because unlike Germaine de Staël, for whom nature remained a dead letter, and who would not have opened her window even to look at the Bay of Naples, Colette's closeness to nature was always sufficient to preserve her from despair.

If we are to find equals for Colette, we must not look for them among women. The themes and preoccupations of her novels deceive us into judging her as if she were exclusively feminine. In reality, what *L'Etoile Vesper* and

[1] *Le Fanal Bleu.*

Le Fanal Bleu show us is the heart of a 'great man' as she had once imagined it beating in her breast. By the resourcefulness and vigour of her mind, by that 'intelligent masculine spirit', she has affinities with Montaigne, as I have already indicated. Their characters have more than one point in common, were it only in the wisdom and moderation with which they were able to regulate their lives, each of them striving for 'the golden mean'. But if Montaigne's 'art of growing old' includes a certain measure of disenchantment, with Colette, on the other hand, the capacity for wonder increases right to the end. In that respect, she no doubt offers us an example unique in the whole history of literature. Where Montaigne, nearing fifty, considered that 'decrepitude is a solitary state', and that 'it is time to turn one's back on company' since 'it is imposing too much on nature to drive it so far that it is compelled to forsake us and abandon our safe conduct to a stranger's aid', Colette merely concludes: 'I can no longer set my steps in the unexpected direction, I must almost give up choosing. . . . I have become dependent on others.' But we see that she is still resourceful enough to turn even this state of dependency to advantage, to discover in her own incapacity a new source of fruitful experience. If she is still able, after innumerable precautions have been taken, to go out for a motor car drive, she at once gives thanks for the good fortune that

L

[161]

enables her to savour the most paradoxical element of our present century: slowness. 'There is so much to look at when one drives slowly,' she remarks. 'All the sharp outlines that speed turns to a blur spring back to life. It has taken me so many years and so many discomforts to gain the right to go slowly, to stop when the fancy takes me, for a narcissus, a purple orchid, a wild strawberry!'[1]

The same old sense of wonderment – that is the only word for it – is still there. As she advances deeper into old age, life seems to her to grow ever richer in various marvels; and for that matter she even tells us explicitly that since old age has endowed her with an even greater faculty for wonder, she considers her 'impediments' are a small price to pay for such a precious gain.

But Colette and Montaigne in old age offer further themes for reflection and contrast. For Montaigne, 'the only consolation of old age is that nature robs us of life by small degrees. When death finally comes it will be by that much less complete and hurtful, since it can kill only the half or the quarter of a man.' This mood of resignation, which, if it does not spring from despair, certainly conveys a despairing note, is completely foreign to Colette, who refused all pain-killing drugs so as to retain full consciousness. She preferred to wage the struggle in full possession of all her faculties. In her view, it was

[1] *Le Fanal Bleu.*

merely a further form of self-enrichment: 'I should hesitate to say they were bad nights, those nights when arthritis decides to torment me in thigh and leg. In the way the pain comes and goes, in short sharp stabs or in waves, there is a certain rhythm that I cannot altogether stigmatize. . . . What I mean by suffering honourably is to meet this embodiment of pain on its own ground. When I stand up, it prevents me from walking, but when I am lying down, I can hold my own against it. . . . Pain, when you torment one of my limbs, I have waited – except in those rare moments when my will has faltered – for you to withdraw, and you have withdrawn. You have not yet been able to make me wake in stupor, with a bitter taste in my mouth, nor troubled my sleep with wan and dubious marvels. . . .'[1] As against Montaigne's cheerless observation: 'Even should I tickle myself, I cannot so easily wring mirth from this miserable body,' Colette declares: 'Mine is a normal old age, therefore one easily moved to gaiety. It is those who are wretched in old age who are abnormal, the sick and the cross-tempered.' But perhaps it is in the light of this final confession, from a man who nevertheless effectively shaped the whole pattern of his life, that the courage and greatness of Colette stand out most clearly: 'Since it is the privilege of the mind to draw compensation from old age,' declares

[1] *L'Etoile Vesper.*

[163]

Montaigne, 'I most heartily counsel it to do so. . . . Yet I fear mind is a traitor; it is bound by such close fraternal links to body that it constantly abandons me to follow body's lead. Try as I will . . . to hold up to it Seneca and Catullus . . . if its companion has colic, it seems mind has it too.'

Colette rejects this predominance of the painful afflictions of the body. She tells herself to think not of Catullus or Seneca, but of the flower-beds of the Palais Royal, of her own sustaining memories, and the delicious feeling of sitting at her window on misty autumn mornings, the mucuous membrane of her nostrils 'as moist as a dog's'.

If she is at times a prey to reflections of a graver sort, their only effect is to fill her with the desire to set all her affairs in order and not to be taken unawares. 'To be on time, to be ready, with everything in order, it all comes to the same thing,' she remarks. In her music-hall days, she showed such punctuality and rigorous discipline in her work that Georges Wague nicknamed her 'What's the time?' Now, Colette recognized, it was 'time to render accounts'. Not, it is true, to a God, but to men. Thus all her purely human activities must be neatly wound up: no debts, tidy drawers, 'all papers carefully sorted'. This was how her virtue manifested itself, in the sense of *virtus* meaning courage.

Certainly no consciously dramatic note intrudes upon

this final phase, only the simple observation: 'How difficult it is to know how to round off one's life. If it is merely a matter of effort, then I am already trying.' One almost expects her to add in her confidential manner: 'There, I have managed it. Don't be afraid. I am already dead.'

The idea of despair seems never to have occurred to her. One would have thought that, so near to the end, she would have given us her final conclusions about life. But for her, no doubt, the only reality transcending man was that of nature herself in all her immensity, nature in whom man, by a loving study of her ways, can participate in his lifetime, before being wholly absorbed by her in death. I say 'no doubt', because Colette herself is silent on the subject of any final interpretation, death being something she had always refused to discuss. However much she may try to 'arouse some small concern in myself for what comes afterwards', she is bound to confess: 'I am not interested in death, nor in my own death either.' But it is in *Le Fanal Bleu* that her admirable detachment from everything concerning her own mortal span is most clearly expressed:

'If our precious senses grow dim with the passing of time, we should not allow that to alarm us unduly. I write "we" but it is really myself I am preaching to. Above all, when I find myself, after a slow progression, arrived at a new stage, I wish to be under no illusion as to its nature. For it has a name. It is not that I rejoice in the fact, but that I have no choice.

'Lifting my eyes a first, a second, a third time from the book or the blue writing paper to the magnificent lawn that is offered to my gaze, I thought: "The children are less noisy in the Gardens this year," then a little later, I accused the front door bell, the telephone, and the full range of orchestral sounds on the radio of gradually fading away. As for the porcelain lamp ... I could only grumble unjustly on its account: "What has it been feeding on to give such a lowered light?" O discoveries, and ever fresh discoveries! It is only a matter of waiting and all becomes clear. Instead of drawing near to the islands, am I not sailing towards that open sea where only the solitary sound of the heart is heard, like the beat of the tide? Nothing perishes, it is I who am drawing away, let us not fear.'[1]

Before a resignation borne so openly and calmly, before such a tranquil acceptance of the inexorable law of nature, one is gripped with respect. In Colette's evolution, everything follows a logical order: she shirks nothing in the working out of a destiny that, in her own eyes, must be finite. And if we consider all the time Colette had, in her hours of pain and insomnia, to reflect

[1] *Le Fanal Bleu.*

[166]

upon the fate that lurks in wait for us all in the un-
fathomable future, it must be admitted that she is the
embodiment of one of the finest forms of stoicism of
which a human is capable.

Here we find no angry outburst, no romantic and in-
dignant appeal to nature because our departure leaves her
indifferent. Colette, on the contrary, draws consolation
from the idea that *everything* will go on just as before when
she has gone. It is a further way of ranging herself
passionately on the side of life, even after her own death.
We see her once more entrench herself more deeply in
what had been one of the primary impulses of her being.
Years before, the heroine of *La Retraite Sentimentale*,
having seen the death of the one she loved, had found
consolation in the spectacle of spring restoring to the
countryside 'the tight, rose-shaped buds of the chestnut
. . . the filigreed cups of wild anemones . . . the sparkling
wine of a new sun . . .', and had drawn fresh strength
from 'all that remains intact, inevitable, unforeseen and
serene in the passage of the hours, in the background of
the seasons. . . .'

Such fidelity to oneself surely allows us to suppose that
Colette was finally able to complete the perfect circle for
which she had always longed, and thus, at the very end of
her life, could tread once more in the steps of the childhood from which all her emotional power and riches

[167]

derived. More than once, she must have experienced that tender hallucination she had already known towards the middle of her life, and which had made her exclaim: 'I recognize the trail that leads back. Many a stage has been passed and left behind. . . . Yet here on earth, when I thought I should no longer follow it this side of the grave, there is still the path through the kitchen garden along which I can retrace my own footprints once more. At the edge of the well, a maternal ghost in an old-fashioned dress of blue satinette is filling the watering cans. That freshness of sparkling water, that gentle lure, that spirit of country ways and innocence, surely these are the charming appeal life makes at its close.'[1]

We seem, indeed, to hear the sound of a flute in an orchard. Some country divinity is offering us the golden apples of a marvellous promise. What we had thought of until now as a disaster – old age and the end that awaits it – is changed for us into a wise and tender harmony. It would be hard to imagine a more total transformation. Who, in the final analysis, is this being who dazzles us with the riches of a last harvest? As silence closed around Colette, we can be certain that she was visited many a time by the maternal phantom in the unforgotten 'dress of satinette'. Strangely, another figure appears at Colette's side, a writer who stood at the opposite pole from her in

[1] *La Naissance du Jour.*

[168]

his conception of life and death, yet the only one who perhaps had a comparable respect and nostalgia for childhood: Georges Bernanos. Bridging the gulf backwards from deathbed to childhood, the childhood we all betray more deeply each year, and recalling the small boy he had once been, the one who seemed to him most dead among all the different persons he had been in the course of his life, Bernanos tells us: 'It is nevertheless the small boy who, when the hour comes, will resume his place at the head of my life, gathering in all my poor years down to the last, and then like a young captain with his veterans, rallying his disordered troops, will enter first into the Father's House.'[1]

For Bernanos, it was an entry into a heavenly kingdom. For Colette, the last hours must have crowded together under her mother's care. It was a return to the maternal breast. For once, the river had succeeded in flowing back to its source.

'That air of impatience, upraised with waiting, that one sees in dead butterflies with wide-stretched wings.' Colette's phrase invincibly suggests what the moment of her own death must have been when, striving to win through to a new freedom, she struggled to escape from the exhausted body. It was on the motionless quivering of the great blue and violet butterflies that gleamed like

[1] *Les Grands Cimetières sous la Lune.*

[169]

enamels in her room that her eyes fell for the last time, while for a listener she could no longer see, she murmured her mother's old imperative, the command full of wonder surging up from the remotest depths of her distant childhood: 'Look!'

IX

Colette and Posterity

Fame is the sun of the dead.

BALZAC

IT is always a moving exercise, whatever the risks of error involved, to try to gauge the future place that the work of a recently dead writer will occupy. At once, light is thrown upon that work from a new angle: that of posterity. It is posterity with its invisible scales that secretly and untiringly examines and weighs the work, and far removed from the judgments of a public concerned only with the immediate, determines the rank that befits a writer, the rank in which he will henceforth be judged with his peers.

Colette is at once a well known and yet a little known writer, in the sense that her novels have won her a reputation as a writer of fiction, to the detriment of the much more profound personality that is revealed as soon as she begins to speak of her childhood, of Sido, of illness or of old age.

The two currents of her work can now be clearly

discerned. One corresponds to those works of pure fiction which illustrate the writer's conception of the relationships between men and women. Whether one is concerned with *Duo*, *Le Toutounier*, *La Seconde*, or *Julie de Carneilhan*, one cannot but judge this the less rich of the two (although an exception must be made for *La Vagabonde*, and above all for *Chéri* and *La Fin de Chéri*). In spite of the popular favour that has been shown for this fictional aspect of Colette's work, it is possible that it will not always retain its hold over the reading public. It is not merely because they belong to a past whose conventions and frivolity seem to us outmoded that a great many of her characters must lose their appeal. The Princesse de Clèves and Julien Sorel also portrayed the conventions of their epoch, yet they remain contemporary by virtue of those emotions that are common to all ages. The more concrete and particularized the character, the more it is likely to avoid being outdated. It is their relative lack of psychological complexity that condemns Colette's heroes, in spite of the number of readers who momentarily see their own reflection in them. One can be certain that any woman will recognize herself in the jealousy of a Madame Farou or a Julie de Carneilhan, where only a small sector of the whole emotional field is explored, but far less certain that any man will recognize himself in the analysis Proust gives of Swann's jealousy, since for that he must share the same subtle and nervous sensibility as Proust's character, the same capacity to people his whole world with the feeling of the beloved's absence. A work only receives its final consecration through the choice of a very restricted number; and it is thus possible to foresee what the judgment of posterity will be.

The second current, on the other hand, introduces us to the real Colette, not so much by a direct account of any particular episode in her life as by the observations, judgments and reactions which she scattered through her writings, and which serve as so many revelations of her deepest being. Unlike the memoir-writers of the seventeenth century, who draw their own portrait in a few lines, or devote to it at most half a page, Colette disseminates the elements of her own character throughout her work. For that matter, she herself puts us on our guard: 'People think I am drawing my own portrait. Be patient: it is only the model for one.'[1] In other words, like those artists whose personality is filtered through their work, she endowed her work with the firm outline that was absent from her life. It is to this exemplary 'model' that we shall refer from now on, when we talk of Colette the writer. In every creative writer, there are really two personalities, the social being whom others apprehend and take to be the whole person, and the deeper per-

[1] *La Naissance du Jour.*

[173]

sonality, out of reach of human relationships and daily events, that labours invisibly, manipulating and reshaping the elements of its own nature, in order to create the spiritual progeny that will alone survive. Colette always refused to write a straightforward autobiography: 'I have tried in the past', she tell us, 'to write my recollections as if all must be divulged, nothing held back. The result was only worth tearing up and throwing away, it savoured of nothing but ill-contrived gossip.'[1] It was because she refused to adopt a wholly subjective approach that the reader finds himself faced with a new task: he must retrace his steps through the novels that at first sight had persuaded him that Colette was an objective writer. Once he perceives those secret signposts that had at first escaped his notice, he will gradually come to recognize the celebrated 'model' that Colette shaped with so much patience, and it is then that he can really come to grips with her work, and compare his own conception of life with hers.

One curious fact is that the dread accolade of massive popular approval has been given to just those aspects of Colette's work that are most likely to endure. It is the Colette who writes of cats and dogs and animals in general, indeed, of the whole world of nature, that the general public has singled out for its praise, and the future

[1] *Le Fanal Bleu.*

[174]

will surely show more and more that it has not been mistaken in its preference.

That is why Colette takes her place among the greatest writers of her generation, even although she is totally unlike some, and yet, paradoxically, has affinities with others from whom, at first glance, she seems farthest removed.

When we look back, for example, at the problems of aesthetics which preoccupied Gide and Valéry in their twenties, in the years around 1890, when the preciosity of certain literary circles even drove the young Gide to write such a sentence as this, on the subject of dreams: 'The abrupt gathering of the chimerical Corymbus' threatens to 'send the petals falling in the cold wind of reality', we can see that such a mode of approach was bound to remain entirely foreign to the spontaneity, even if severely controlled, of a Colette, whose talent sprang up like a healthy young plant growing wild. In the same way, she could never have delivered herself of such a remark as Gide's to Valéry: 'You are right, Paul Ambroise: we must start from the assumption that, after all, living is not really necessary.' And it is here that we can perceive a resemblance, highly disconcerting at first glance, but certainly valid at least in terms of temperament, between Colette and another writer who also drew his strength from his native countryside: Paul Claudel. Both of them preserved the same close contact with the soil, and thus avoided any risk of succumbing to that form of intellectualism that went as far as to question the very value of life itself. In both, one finds the same love of the fruits of the earth, the same equilibrium, the same eagerness to share in every manifestation of nature, which showed itself in their common taste for tales of travel. 'When I was still a child,' Colette tells us, 'I was already a great traveller. I followed almost the same paths and the same guides as I do today. I would open one of the volumes of the *Tour du Monde*, and return only when I had visited some part of the Universe.'[1] For Claudel, it was above all Jules Verne who showed the way to far-off wonders. But if the young Claudel was seeking to satisfy not only a passion for the exotic, but a violent need for action as well, Colette's aim, as she followed her explorers, was to gather the fabulous flowers of the tropics, or gaze at some insect only to be found on the banks of the Amazon.

A passage from Claudel shows us that his sense of curiosity was just as lively as the young Colette's, although the direction he gave to it was very different: 'I can see myself once more on the highest branch of the old tree shaken by the wind, a child poised aloft among the apples. From there, like a God upon his stem, a spectator looking

[1] *Mélanges.*

[176]

down upon the theatre of the world in a profound
contemplation, I studied the outlines and conformation of
the earth, the disposition of slopes and planes; eye un-
winking as a crow's, I scanned the countryside spread out
beneath my perch.'

Where Claudel, in a rather solemn tone, speaks of
'profound contemplation', Colette describes, for example,
'the fantastic sprouting of the mushroom which, as it
grows taller, raises aloft on its round head the leaf that
saw it born', or 'the sound of an insect's delicate foot, or
irises unfolding', since her only ambition is to add
her 'slender contribution to the treasury of human knowledge'.

It is nevertheless true that both writers share a delight
in exploiting all that is magnificently and innocently
offered in the realm of nature. But Fère-en-Tardenois, set
in the flat Champagne country where the winds of heaven
blow freely and there is nothing to arrest the eye, bred in
the young Claudel the habit of gazing out upon vast
spaces; while Saint-Sauveur-en-Puisaye, among the
charming folds of its hills, gave Colette her slightly
myopic gaze, which sees everything near at hand and
magnifies the detail of anything she is contemplating.
Unlike, also, Colette's free-thinking parents and the irreverent ways of her native village, Claudel's family on
their Champagne estate, the air resounding with church

bells, were steeped in Christian traditions. And the poet's conversion was to divert a part of his passion into a very different channel from the wholly physical course it had taken until that moment.

These similarities of temperament are therefore only applicable to the period of their youth. It happens that two rivers may have their source almost at the same point; but their course gradually takes them farther and farther apart; and at their mouths they have arrived at entirely different destinations. Thus it was with Colette and Claudel at the moment of their death. Within the space of a year, the catafalque erected on the parvis of Notre Dame, invoking the prayers of the faithful and the blessings of the Church, and that other catafalque, displayed in the gardens of the Palais Royal, and appealing only to the gratitude of men, bring finally home to us the fundamental opposition between these two great contemporaries.

*   *   *

At the moment of bidding farewell to Colette, who like all creators preserves intact the one great and essential mystery, the mystery of her genius, which was something that concerned only her and the ineffable, if we try to add one final touch to the portrait, we may recall what Proust said of Ruskin: 'In death, he continues to cast his radiance upon us, like those extinguished stars whose light still reaches us, and it is through his eyes, now closed forever in the depths of the tomb, that generations yet to be born will look upon Nature.'

Bibliography

In the following bibliography, an asterisk preceding a title indicates that it has appeared in English translation. The principal English translations are listed separately at the end.

Claudine à l'Ecole, by Willy. Paris, 1900: P. Ollendorff. Colette's name in association with Willy's appears only in editions published after 1911.

Claudine à Paris, by Willy. Paris, 1901: Ollendorff. Colette's name in association with Willy's appears only in editions published after 1911.

Claudine en Ménage, by Willy. Paris, 1902: Mercure de France. Colette's name in association with Willy's appears only in editions published after 1924.

Claudine en Ménage, by Willy. Paris, 1902: Mercure de France. Colette's name in association with Willy's appears only in editions published after 1924.

Claudine s'en va, by Willy. Paris, 1903: P. Ollendorff. Colette's name in association with Willy's appears only in editions published after 1907.

Minne, by Willy. Paris, 1904: P. Ollendorff.

Les Egarements de Minne, by Willy. Paris, 1905: Ollendorff.

(The two preceding works, much altered and recast in a single volume, were published under the signature of Colette Willy in 1909, under the new title of *L'Ingénue libertine*.)

*Dialogues de Bêtes, by Colette Willy. Paris, 1904: Mercure de France. The 1904 edition contained only four stories In 1907, a new edition appeared containing seven stories, and with a preface by Francis Jammes.

La Retraite Sentimentale, by Colette Willy. Paris, 1907: Mercure de France.

Les Vrilles de la Vigne, by Colette Willy. Paris, 1908: Editions de la Vie Parisienne.

*L'Ingénue libertine, by Colette Willy. Paris, 1909: P. Ollendorff.

*La Vagabonde, by Colette Willy. Paris, 1911: P. Ollendorff.

Prrou, Poucette et quelques autres, by Colette Willy. Paris, 1913: Librairie des Lettres.

From this point on, all the works listed appeared under Colette's name alone.

L'Envers du Music-Hall. Paris, 1913: Flammarion.

*L'Entrave. Paris, 1913: Librairie des Lettres.

La Paix chez les Bêtes. Paris, 1916: Georges Crès et Cie.

Les Heures longues. Paris, 1917: A. Fayard.

Les Enfants dans les Ruines. Paris, 1917: Editions de la Maison du Livre.

Dans la Foule. Paris, 1918: Georges Crès et Cie.

Mitsou ou comment l'esprit vient aux Filles. Paris, 1919: A. Fayard.

La Chambre éclairée. Paris, 1920: Edouard Joseph.

Chéri. Paris, 1920: A Fayard.

La Maison de Claudine. Paris, 1922: J. Ferenczi.

Le Voyage égoiste. Paris, 1922: Edouard Pelletan.

Le Blé en herbe. Paris, 1923: Flammarion.

Rêverie de Nouvel An. Paris, 1925: Stock.

La Femme Cachée. Paris, 1924: Flammarion.

Aventures quotidiennes. Paris, 1924: Flammarion.

Quatre Saisons. Paris, 1925: Philippe Ortiz.

La Fin de Chéri. Paris, 1926: Flammarion.

La Naissance du Jour. Paris, 1928: Flammarion.

Renée Vivien. Abbeville, 1928: F. Paillart.

La Seconde. Paris, 1929: J. Ferenczi.

Sido. Paris, 1929: Editions Krâ.

Histoires pour Bel Gazou. Paris, 1930: Stock.

Supplément à Don Juan. Paris, 1931: Editions du Trianon.

Paradis terrestre. Lausanne, 1932: Gonin et Cie.

Prisons et Paradis. Paris, 1932: J. Ferenczi.

Ces Plaisirs. Paris, 1932: J. Ferenczi. This work was reprinted in 1941 under the title *Le Pur et l'Impur*.

La Chatte. Paris, 1933: B. Grasset.

Duo. Paris, 1934: J. Ferenczi.

La Jumelle Noire. Paris, 1934, 1935, 1937, 1938: J. Ferenczi. A collection of dramatic criticisms.

Discours de réception à l'Académie Royale de Belgique. Paris, 1936: B. Grasset.

★Mes Apprentissages. Paris, 1936: J. Ferenczi.

Chats. Paris, 1936: Jacques Nam.

Splendeur des Papillons. Text by Colette. Paris, 1937: Plon.

Bella-Vista. Paris, 1937: J. Ferenczi.

Le Toutounier. Paris, 1939: J. Ferenczi.

Chambre d'Hôtel. Paris, 1940: A. Fayard.

Journal à Rebours. Paris, 1941: A. Fayard.

★Julie de Carneilhan. Paris, 1941: A. Fayard.

De ma fenêtre. Paris, 1942: Aux Armes de France.

De la Patte à l'Aile. Paris, 1943: Corrêa.

Flore et Pomone. Paris, 1943: Editions de la Galerie Charpentier.

Nudité. Paris, 1943: Editions de la Mappemonde.

Le Képi. Paris, 1943: A. Fayard.

Broderie ancienne. Monaco, 1941: Editions du Rocher.

★Gigi. Lausanne 1944: La Guilde du Livre.

Trois, Six, Neuf. Paris, 1944: Editions Corrêa.

Belles Saisons. Paris, 1945: Editions de la Galerie Charpentier.

Une Amitié inattendue. Correspondence of Colette with Francis Jammes. Paris, 1945: Emile Paul Frères.

L'Etoile Vesper. Geneva, 1946: Editions du Milieu du Monde.

En Camarade. A play in two acts. Paris, 1948: Société d'Imprimerie Parisienne.

Pour un Herbier. Lausanne 1948: Mermod.

Trait pour Trait. Paris, 1949: Le Fleuron.

[184]

Journal intermittent. Paris, 1949: Le Fleuron.

Le Fanal Bleu. Paris, 1949: J. Ferenczi.

La Fleur de l'Age. Paris, 1949: Le Fleuron.

En Pays connu. Paris, 1949: Manuel Bruker.

Chats de Colette. Paris, 1949: Albin Michel.

A stage version of *Chéri*, written in collaboration with Léopold Marchand. Paris, 1922: Librairie Théâtrale.

A stage version of *La Vagabonde*, written in collaboration with Léopold Marchand. Paris, 1923: Imprimerie de l'Illustration. A. Chatenet.

Colette also wrote a lyrical fantasy for the musical score of Maurice Ravel's *L'Enfant et les Sortilèges*. Paris, 1925: Durand et Cie.

The Complete Works of Colette were published in the Editions du Fleuron, by Flammarion in 1950.

Colette's works in English translation:

Recaptured (L'Entrave). Translated by Viola Gerard Garvin. Gollancz. 1931.

Mitsou or how girls grow wise (Mitsou). Translated by Jane Terry. Gollancz. 1930.

The Mother of Claudine (La Maison de Claudine). Translated by Charles King. Werner Laurie. 1937.

The Ripening Corn (Le Blé en herbe). Translated by Phyllis Mégroz. Gollancz. 1931.

Morning Glory (La Naissance du Jour). Translated by Rosemary Benét. Gollancz. 1932.

Fanny and Jane (La Seconde). Translated by Viola Gerard Garvin. Gollancz. 1931.

Saha the Cat (La Chatte). Translated by Morris Bentinck. Werner Laurie. 1936.

The Married Lover (Duo). Translated by Marjorie Laurie. Werner Laurie. 1935.

In addition to the above, Secker and Warburg are at present engaged on issuing a collected edition of Colette's works in English, of which the following volumes have so far appeared:

Chéri and *The Last of Chéri*. Translated by Roger Senhouse. 1951.

Creatures Great and Small. Translated by Enid McLeod. 1951.

Julie de Carneilhan and *Chance Acquaintances*. Translated by Patrick Leigh Fermor. 1952.

My Mother's House. Translated by Una Vicenzo Troubridge and Enid McLeod. 1953.

Sido. Translated by Enid McLeod. 1953.

Gigi. Translated by Roger Senhouse. 1953.

The Cat. Translated by Antonia White. 1953.

The Vagabond. Translated by Enid McLeod. 1954.

Ripening Seed. Translated by Roger Senhouse. 1955.

Claudine at School. Translated by Antonia White. 1956.